before

Infancy

Guest Editors

George E. Butterworth

Department of Psychology, University of Southampton

and

Paul L. Harris

Department of Experimental Psychology, Oxford

The British Psychological Society

Published by The British Psychological Society.
Headquarters St Andrews House, 48 Princess Road East, Leicester LE1 7DR, UK.
Distribution Centre Blackhorse Road, Letchworth, Herts SG6 1HN.

First published without an index in *British Journal of Developmental Psychology*, volume 3, September 1985—a publication of The British Psychological Society.

ISBN 0 901715 47 6

Printed in Great Britain by Latimer Trend & Company Ltd, Plymouth.

Contents*

*Page numbers all refer to the numbers in square brackets at the head of every page.

British Journal of Developmental Psychology (1985), **3**, 209–210   *Printed in Great Britain*

Editorial

Research on human infancy during the past quarter of a century has made a fundamental contribution to our understanding of development. One of the most significant results has been to transform our theories of how knowledge is acquired. In the late 1950s, there were two broad theoretical positions. The first assumed that any change that occurred during infancy was a consequence of maturation. The second assumed that the infant was more or less a blank slate with a great deal to learn, though the exact mode of learning was left unspecified. Extensive research on the nature of perception in infants, on how infants acquire control over action, on their understanding of objects and space has led to a fundamental reappraisal. Infants come into the world with a much richer repertoire for acting and perceiving than the empiricist view had led us to believe. On the other hand, their capacity to remember and to learn from experience is much more powerful than the maturational account ever acknowledged.

The impact of these discoveries continues to generate considerable tension for those concerned with epistemological issues. On the one hand, the neonate is equipped with mechanisms for detecting and interpreting perceptual input in a veridical fashion. On the other hand, infants persist in various mistakes when attempting to solve apparently simple sensorimotor problems. Such mistakes betray their intellectual naïveté. One important question then that continues to preoccupy researchers in infancy is how to reconcile the perceptual sophistication of the neonate with the intellectual apprenticeship he or she manifestly undertakes in the course of the first 18 months. This tension is reflected in our special issue. Papers by Slater, Morison, Town & Rose, by Samuels & Ewy and by Hainline & Lemerise provide new evidence and a critical review of the perceptual competence of the neonate. In contrast, papers by Wishart & Bower and by Willatts underline the persisting naïveté of the infant, albeit a naïveté that appropriate training can dramatically curtail. Piéraut-Le Bonniec bridges these two themes with an illustration of the way in which a perceptual distinction—between convexity and concavity—is only slowly used to guide appropriate action.

A second major result of research on infancy is a new conception of the social competence of the baby. The baby is no longer seen as a passive recipient of mother love but as a participant in an evolving dialogue. Preverbal infants are equipped with various mechanisms for communication with caretakers. They engage in a non-verbal exchange that depends upon a subtle alternation of watching and turn taking. They are able to imitate the gestures of a caretaker. They are able to use a caretaker's direction of gaze and pointing gestures to guide their own attention. Having said that, the point of departure for this dialogue and the mechanism by which it evolves into a symbolic exchange remain controversial issues. Three of the papers add fuel to this controversy. Sylvester-Bradley argues that differential reactions to persons vs. inanimate objects do not constitute evidence for an innate acknowledgement that people are special types of objects. Zinober & Martlew argue that the shift from 'accidental' to 'intentional' dialogue is a long and gradual process. Finally, Lewis, Sullivan & Brooks-Gunn demonstrate that the infant's persistence and emotional stability are keenly affected by the extent to which changes in the environment are contingent upon the infant's efforts. Lewis, Sullivan & Brooks-Gunn do not set their demonstration in the context of the dialogue between infant and caretaker, but the implications of their work for the sustenance of that dialogue are clear enough.

That we have been able to devote a special issue of the *British Journal of Developmental Psychology* to research on human infancy, with many more papers submitted than there is space available, shows that the field continues to flourish. The papers reflect an international community of researchers, all aware that work in human infancy is at the cutting edge of scientific psychology. If we want to understand human development, we need to know how it originates.

The special issue would not have been possible without the help of many other people. We would like to thank Vicky Phillips and Peter Bryant for smoothing the editorial process. Finally we would like to express our appreciation to the reviewers; we badgered some of them mercilessly with manuscript after manuscript, revision after revision, and even after that we occasionally had the gall to disagree with them.

Paul L. Harris   George E. Butterworth

British Journal of Developmental Psychology (1985), **3**, 211–220   *Printed in Great Britain*

Movement perception and identity constancy in the new-born baby

Alan Slater, Victoria Morison, Carole Town and David Rose

Five experiments using the visual preference method (Expt 1) and an infant-controlled habituation procedure (Expts 2–5) are described. Their aim was to examine the salience of movement, both rotation and translation, as a stimulus for new-borns, and to investigate under what conditions information about shape can be extracted from stationary and moving stimuli. A moving stimulus, whether rotating or translating, was found to be consistently preferred to an identical stationary stimulus (Expt 1). Following habituation to one direction of rotation, no novelty preferences were found for the other direction of rotation (Expt 2); this suggests that clockwise and anticlockwise movements may be comparable for the new-born.

The other experiments suggest that new-borns can extract shape information from stationary and moving stimuli, and can transfer what is learned to moving and to stationary stimuli (Expts 3 and 5). This transfer occurred when (*a*) the spatiotemporal changes caused by stimulus rotation were the same from habituation to post-criterion trials (Expt 3), and (*b*) orientation did not change (due to the use of translation movement) across conditions (Expt 5). There was no evidence that new-borns could transfer learning from stationary to rotating stimuli or vice versa (Expt 4).

This demonstrates that new-borns can perceive a similarity between a stimulus when moving and when stationary, and suggests a degree of visual organization that is not usually attributed to the new-born: Expt 5 in particular suggests that the perceptual potential for identity constancy is present from birth.

Movement is a powerful dimension of visual stimulation for the human infant. From 2 weeks of age infants prefer to fixate or scan moving rather than stationary representations of human faces (Wilcox & Clayton, 1968; Carpenter, 1974), and prefer a rotating yellow and red disc to a stationary complex three-dimensional shape (Fantz & Nevis, 1967). Older infants of 1, 2 and 3 months have been shown to prefer horizontally oscillating checkerboards to stationary ones (Volkmann & Dobson, 1976). Nine- and 16-week-old infants prefer a rotating black and white Maltese cross to a stationary one (McKenzie & Day, 1976). The salience of movement as a stimulus dimension is further demonstrated by its capacity to increase the effective visual field both radially (Tronick, 1972) and along the line of regard (McKenzie & Day, 1976).

Because movement elicits strong responses from infants it is important to study specific characteristics of their motion perception. The type of movement, lateral or rotating, and speed of movement are of particular interest. Infants aged 1, 2 and 3 months behave differentially towards a laterally oscillating stimulus when paired with a stationary one. This provides cues for an observer to identify which of two stimuli is moving, and these cues become more reliable as the rate of movement increases up to a value of about 90 cycles/minute, and then they become less reliable (Volkmann & Dobson, 1976). This observation suggests that an increase in speed up to 90 cycles/minute makes movement a more salient or attractive stimulus for infants within this age range. For rotating stimuli, infants 8 to 20 weeks old prefer a faster (84°/second) to a slower (47°/second) rotation, and the slower rotation to the same stimulus when stationary (Burnham & Day, 1979).

If movement is a salient stimulus that is detected and responded to in a way other than just as an automatic reflexive response, then we may expect infants to detect properties of the stimulus other than movement, i.e. colour and form. Bower, however, has claimed that infants less than 20 weeks of age do not detect these properties of moving objects but simply respond to the movement *per se* of the object, and this is perceived as something quite different from the same object when stationary (Bower, 1971, 1974; Bower *et al.*, 1971; Bower & Paterson, 1973). According to this view, when infants are presented with a moving object that stops, the infants think the stationary object is a new object and, conversely, they do not identify a stationary object with itself when moving.

However, more recently it has been shown that 10-week-old infants who have been operantly trained to discriminate between a cube and sphere when stationary maintain this discrimination when the objects are moving (Hartlep & Forsyth, 1977). In addition, 8–20-week-old infants have been shown to transfer discriminations of colour between stationary and moving, moving and stationary, and between fast and slow rotating conditions (Burnham & Day, 1979). These two studies show that infants from 2 months can extract colour and shape information from moving objects. The reason why Bower did not find evidence for this capacity may be due to the type of movement that was used: the stimuli in Bower's experiments moved laterally over a fairly large area, whereas Hartlep & Forsyth and Burnham & Day used circular or rotating movement.

The importance of the type of movement is demonstrated in a study by Ruff (1982). Object recognition was generally improved by movement for 6-month-olds. However, if the movement was a continuous transformation from one orientation to the next, i.e. a rotating type of movement, the infants were unable to extract shape information from the moving object; movement that involved small changes of location but no change in orientation, i.e. translation, was most effective in aiding detection of the object structure.

There are no reports of the new-born's ability to extract shape, direction of movement, or other information from moving objects. The purpose of the experiments described here was twofold: first to examine the salience of rotation and translation as stimuli for new-borns (Expts 1 and 2); second, to investigate if, and under what conditions, shape can be extracted from moving and stationary stimuli, and also whether what is learned will transfer both within (Expt 3) and between (Expts 4 and 5) moving and stationary conditions. The two types of movement used, rotation and translation, were selected with the constraints of testing new-borns in mind, and the rationale for their selection is described in the General method section.

There are two theoretical positions making competing predictions as to the results that might be obtained. According to the first, there is a qualitative change in looking behaviour occurring around 6–8 weeks from birth; prior to this age infants should be unable to extract meaningful information from visual stimulation (Bronson, 1974, 1982; Maurer & Lewis, 1979). According to the second view, developmental changes in visual perceptual abilities are primarily quantitative in nature, and the new-born differs from older infants in his or her poorer information-processing abilities (Aronson & Tronick, 1971; Werner & Perlmutter, 1979; Antell & Keating, 1983).

Five experiments are described here—the first using the visual preference method, the others using a habituation procedure—that explore these issues using new-borns as subjects. The procedures and stimuli used are described next.

General method

Subjects

Subjects for the experiments were 65 full-term new-born babies, 36 males and 29 females, mean age 3 days 9 hours (range 7 hours to 11 days 15 hours). A further 45 babies were seen but could not be used as subjects for the following reasons: failure to habituate ($n=2$); sleeping, crying or fussing ($n=31$); position bias on the critical trials ($n=12$). On the critical trials (described below) 40 s fixation to paired stimuli was the dependent variable, and subjects were excluded on the grounds of position bias if 35 s or more were spent fixating the stimulus on one side only. All subjects were normal, healthy babies, and no infant with birth complications, or real or suspected medical problems, was used.

No baby was habituated to more than one stimulus, but following habituation and post-criterion novelty testing in one experimental condition the same subject, if alert, was often tested in one or more (a maximum of two) of the visual preference conditions of Expt 1. However, no baby was tested in a visual preference condition where prior habituation to a stimulus or to a particular speed of movement could have affected the results. Thus, no baby was tested in a preference condition with the same stimulus, or the same speed of rotation, as that shown on habituation trials.

Subjects were selected from the maternity ward of the Royal Devon and Exeter Hospital, Heavitree, Devon, and were chosen only if they were spontaneously alert. Throughout testing they remained in the behavioural state of alert inactivity (Ashton, 1973).

Stimuli

The stimuli are shown in Fig. 1. They were a Maltese cross, a triangle and a cross. The stimuli were presented against a white background, and were illuminated by striplights placed behind and to both sides of the infant. The luminances of the light background and of the dark figures were, respectively, 137 and 21 cd/m^2. Each stimulus was 12·7 cm high and subtended a visual angle of 23° at the viewing distance of 30 cm. The stimuli were presented either singly (habituation trials of Expts 2–5, described below), or paired together both (*a*) on the post-criterion trials following habituation, and (*b*) for the visual preference studies of Expt 1. During habituation the single stimulus was in the centre of the stimulus screen, and for paired presentation the two stimuli were equidistant from centre and separated by 9 cm. When presented to the subjects one or both of the stimuli were either stationary or undergoing rotation or translation. The differences in stimulus presentation are described in more detail in each of the experiments.

Procedure

The general procedure was the same throughout. Each subject was brought to the experimental room, on the maternity ward of the hospital, and positioned seated upright on one experimenter's knee, with his/her eyes 30 cm (±3 cm) from the stimulus screen. This experimenter was blind to the presented displays throughout the testing. A Rustrak four-channel event-recorder was used, in conjunction with a millisecond timer, to record the duration and direction of the infants' fixations. The procedural details differed for the visual preference studies and for the habituation experiments and these are described next.

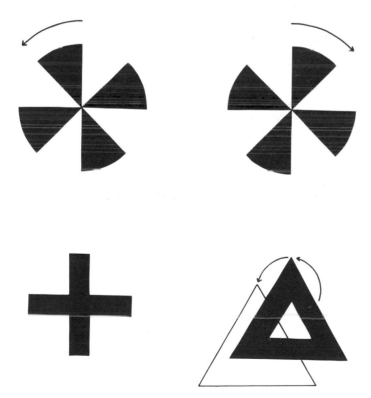

Figure 1. The stimuli and the types of movement used.

Visual preference studies.   Several studies are described under Expt 1. In each of these two paired stimuli were shown to the subjects for two trials, the presentation being the same as described below for the post-criterion trials of the habituation experiments.

Habituation experiments.   In each of Expts 2–5 an infant control procedure was used (Horowitz *et al.*, 1972; Slater *et al.*, 1982, 1983*a, b*, 1984*a, b*). The habituating stimulus was presented and the first trial began when the baby looked: the trial ended with a continuous look away from the stimulus of 2 s or more. The next trial began with the next look, and trials continued until the total of any three consecutive trials, from the fourth trial on, was 50 per cent or less than the total of the first three. Two post-criterion trials were then presented. On each of these the habituated stimulus was paired with the novel stimulus and the trial continued until 20 s of looking had accumulated. The left/right positions of novel and familiar stimuli were reversed from Trial 1 to Trial 2. Complete counterbalancing of habituating stimulus, direction of rotation (clockwise/anticlockwise), and left/right positioning of stimuli on the first post-criterion trial, was used throughout.

For 44 preferential looking trials, and for 28 post-criterion trials, two independent observers recorded the infants' fixations on each of the paired stimuli. The inter-observer agreement was high (Pearson $rs = 0.921$ and 0.892, respectively).

Types of movement

Choice of stimulus movement was determined by constraints on new-born tracking behaviour. In the first few postnatal weeks tracking of a laterally (horizontally) moving stimulus is jerky rather than smooth, consisting often of saccadic 're-capture' motions (Aslin, 1981; Bronson, 1982, p. 91). Given such tracking limitations, it is not clear how any habituation to such a stimulus might be measured. Two types of movement were used which kept the stimulus in approximately the same location: (1) clockwise/anticlockwise rotation in the fronto-parallel plane around the mid-point, Expts 1, 2, 3 and 4 (depicted in the top half of Fig. 1—these Maltese cross stimuli were used only in Expts 1 and 2); (2) clockwise/anticlockwise translation, Expts 1 and 5 depicted at the bottom right of Fig. 1. During translation each part of the stimulus described a circle, with diameter of rotation 6·4 cm. Thus during translation the whole stimulus moved but without changing its orientation. Speed or rotation/translation varied for the preferences of Expt 1 and the variations are described under that experiment; a constant speed of rotation of 45°/s was used throughout Expts 2–5.

The motors that moved the displays made a slight but, to the adult, detectable sound: sound quality did not vary perceptibly with speed or type of movement. To remove auditory localizing cues in those conditions of Expt 1 where moving and stationary stimuli were presented side by side, the motors on both sides were switched on.

Experiment 1

Since there is little research on new-borns' response to movement, the present experiment was carried out to see what preferences exist for movement, for different speeds of rotation, and to ensure that the moving stimuli used in the later experiments could be discriminated from their stationary counterparts.

Method

Subjects.   Subjects were 34 new-borns, 20 males and 14 females, mean age 3 days, range 7 hours to 11 days 15 hours. Of the total, 12 subjects were tested in two conditions, so that there were eight subjects in each of the first five conditions and six in the last.

Procedure.   The six paired stimulus preferential looking conditions were as follows:

(1) rotating (R) 45°/s paired with (p.w.) an identical stationary Maltese cross stimulus;
(2) R Maltese cross 45°/s p.w. R 90°/s;
(3) R Maltese cross 90°/s p.w. R 180°/s;
(4) R Maltese cross 180°/s p.w. stationary stimulus;
(5) R triangle or cross 45°/s p.w. stationary stimulus;
(6) translating triangle or cross 45°/s p.w. stationary stimulus.

The order of presentation of the stimulus pairs was completely counterbalanced with respect to left/right positioning and direction of rotation or translation on the first of the two trials: these were both changed on Trial 2. Maltese cross stimuli were used in conditions (1)–(4). For each of conditions (5) and (6), half the subjects were shown the rotating or translating triangle paired with an identical stationary triangle; half were shown the cross in the same paired conditions.

Results and discussion

The results are presented in Table 1. No preference was found for either of the two slowest speeds of rotation [condition (2)], while the intermediate speed (90°/s) was preferred to the

Table 1. Results of preference studies Expt 1

Condition	n	Stimuli	Non-preferred[a]	Preferred[a]	Mean per cent preference	t value	Significance level[b] P
1	8	Maltese cross	S	R45°/s	66·4	3·89	<0·01
2	8	Maltese cross	R45°/s	R90°/s	53·3	0·67	n.s.
3	8	Maltese cross	R180°/s	R90°/s	61·7	3·34	<0·02
4	8	Maltese cross	S	R180°/s	69·1	3·47	<0·02
5	8	Triangle/cross	S	R45°/s	77·5	4·60	<0·01
6	6	Triangle/cross	S	T45°/s	66·2	4·54	<0·01

[a] S = stationary, R = rotating, T = translating.
[b] All Ps two-tailed.

fastest [180°/s, condition (3)]. At the fastest speed of rotation, and in all other conditions, the moving stimulus was strongly preferred to the identical stationary stimulus.

The results confirm the attention-getting properties of movement, both rotation and translation, for the new-born. The preference for the intermediate, when paired with the fastest speed of rotation, suggests that perhaps at the faster speeds the limits of new-borns' abilities to process the information contained in the stimulus are being reached. Accordingly, rotation/translation of 45°/s was used in Expts 2–5.

Experiment 2

The purpose of this experiment was to ascertain whether new-borns discriminate between direction of rotation.

Method

Subjects.   The subjects were 12 new-borns, six males and six females, mean age 3 days 0·5 hours, range 21 hours to 6 days 4 hours.

Procedure.   The Maltese cross stimuli were used (Fig. 1). Half of the subjects were habituated to the stimulus rotating in a clockwise direction, half to anticlockwise rotation. Following habituation, the post-criterion trials were paired presentation of clockwise and anticlockwise rotating Maltese crosses. Thus the novel stimulus was identical to the habituated one, but opposite in its direction of rotation. Throughout, the speed of rotation was 45°/s (i.e. one cycle every 8 s).

Results and discussion

The infants habituated to the stimuli with a mean total fixation time (TFT) of 133·8 s, range 71·5–271·5; the mean number of trials to criterion was 7·2, range 6 9. On the post-criterion trials no novelty preference was observed: overall 53 per cent of the looking time was spent viewing the novel stimulus (t = 0·67, n.s.).

The absence of novelty preferences following habituation to one direction of rotation cannot be interpreted as an inability to discriminate clockwise from anticlockwise; it might be, for instance, that the difference is detected but is not of sufficient relevance or salience for novelty preferences to emerge. It does mean, though, that both directions can be treated as comparable, and the results are evidence that new-borns reliably habituate to these types of movement. In each of the moving conditions described in Expts 3, 4 and 5 below, half of the subjects were shown clockwise, half anticlockwise, movement.

Experiment 3

If subjects are able to extract or process shape information from a moving stimulus and transfer this discrimination to the stimulus when stationary (and vice versa), two prerequisite conditions would need to be met: firstly, that they are able to discriminate between stationary shapes, and, secondly, that they can discriminate between moving shapes. The first of these has been demonstrated with new-borns (Slater *et al.*, 1983*a*); the second was investigated in this experiment.

Method

Subjects.   The subjects were eight new-borns, four males and four females, mean age 3 days 9 hours, range 20 hours to 8 days 23 hours.

Procedure.   The stimuli were the cross and triangle shown in Fig. 1. Rotation rather than the translation movement of the triangle shown in Fig. 1 was used in this experiment. These stimuli were chosen because they have approximately the same contour density while being clearly different from each other. Half of the subjects were habituated to the rotating triangle, the others to the rotating cross. Following habituation the post-criterion trials were paired presentation of both stimuli, both rotating in the same direction as the habituated stimulus.

Results and discussion

The results, given by subjects and stimulus conditions, are shown in Table 2. The subjects habituated to each of the stimuli, and there were no obvious differences between the stimuli on habituation trials. A very strong novelty preference was found, and no subject spent more time looking at the familiar stimulus on the post-criterion trials.

   These results clearly demonstrate that new-borns are able to extract at least some shape information from a moving stimulus, and that this information transfers from habituation to post-habituation trials. What is not clear is whether or not the stimulus details encoded depend upon the spatiotemporal changes displayed during rotation, or whether this information will transfer from a moving to a stationary display, or vice versa. These questions were addressed in the next two experiments.

Experiment 4

One possibility is that the shape information learned from the habituating stimuli of Expt 3 and which permits the strong novelty preferences to emerge, is quite global or non-specific. It might be that infants are born with the capacity to tell the difference between a light area in the centre surrounded by a dark area (the triangle), and a pattern where the dark area is in the centre and the light area around the outside (the cross). If this were the case then the introduction of movement in Expt 3 would be quite immaterial to what is learned; indeed, one would get equally strong novelty preferences on post-criterion testing if the stimulus conditions changed from stationary to moving or vice versa.

   These possibilities were tested in this experiment and in Expt 5. In this experiment two habituation studies are described. In the first (4*a*) rotating stimuli were shown on the post-criterion trials following habituation to a stationary stimulus, and in the second (4*b*) stationary stimuli were shown following habituation to a rotating one.

Method

Subjects.   Subjects were 16 new-borns, 11 males and five females, mean age 3 days 3 hours, range 7 hours to 7 days 22 hours. Eight subjects were tested in each of conditions 4*a* and 4*b*.

Procedure.   In condition 4*a*, half of the subjects were habituated to the stationary cross, half to the stationary triangle. Following habituation, they were given paired presentation of triangle and cross, both rotating in the same direction (either clockwise or anticlockwise). Since the post-criterion stimuli were rotating it is unlikely that the familiar stimulus was in precisely the habituated orientation when the infant first looked at it. In condition 4*b* half the subjects were habituated to the rotating triangle, half to the rotating cross. Following habituation they were given paired presentation of triangle and cross, both stationary.

Results and discussion

A breakdown of the results across conditions is given in Table 3. The finding of interest is that no consistent novelty preferences emerged in either condition: 10 of the 16 subjects looked more at the novel stimulus (five in each condition), but only four of these preferences were greater than 60 per cent.

Table 2. Habituation trials and novelty preferences, Expt 3

Subject	Familiarized stimulus	Direction of rotation	Trials to criterion	Total fixation time (s)	Per cent novelty preference
1	Cross	Anticlockwise	9	130·5	66·2
2	Cross	Anticlockwise	6	78·5	66·2
3	Cross	Clockwise	6	223·0	50·0
4	Cross	Clockwise	6	218·5	70·0
5	Triangle	Anticlockwise	6	69·0	72·5
6	Triangle	Anticlockwise	6	103·5	53·8
7	Triangle	Clockwise	6	90·5	68·8
8	Triangle	Clockwise	6	156·0	75·0
		Average	6·4	133·7	65·3[a]

[a] $t = 4·89$, d.f. $= 7$, $P < 0·005$, one-tailed.

These results, taken together with those from Expt 3, suggest that the stimulus changes that accompany rotation are responded to by new-borns. The major implication of the results is that the shift from stationary to rotating stimuli (condition 4a), and vice versa (4b), from the habituation to the post-criterion trials makes both of the paired post-criterion stimuli novel, in both conditions. It may be that some components of the 'familiar' post-criterion stimulus are detected on the post-criterion trials, but not responded to in a consistent fashion because of its additional novelty value. However, it might equally be the case that moving and stationary stimuli are perceived as quite different objects or shapes by new-borns. These differences in interpretation cannot be resolved by the null results of this experiment, given that the potentially confounding factor of continuous orientation changes accompanied the rotating, but not the stationary, stimuli. In order to clarify interpretation the last experiment used moving stimuli whose orientation remained constant.

Table 3. Habituation trials and novelty preferences, Expt 4

Stimuli[a]		No. of subjects	Mean no. of trials to criterion	Mean total fixation time (s)	Mean per cent novelty preference
Familiar	Novel				
Condition 4a					
Cross S	Triangle R	4	6·25	74·6	53·5
Triangle S	Cross R	4	6·5	113·9	53·1
Average			6·4	94·2	53·3**
Condition 4b					
Cross R	Triangle S	4	6·5	119·6	61·2
Triangle R	Cross S	4	8·0	111·6	49·4
Average			7·2	115·6	55·3***
Overall average			6·8	104·9	54·3****

$t = 0·52$; *$t = 0·7$; ****$t = 0·9$.
[a] S = stationary, R = rotating.

Experiment 5

The experimental conditions were similar to those of Expt 4, the difference being that the stimulus movement was translation rather than rotation. The translation movement was described earlier, and illustrated in Fig. 1: during translation the whole stimulus moved, but without changing its orientation. New-born infants discriminate translating stimuli from, and prefer them to, equivalent stationary forms (Expt 1).

Method

Subjects.   Subjects were 16 new-borns, 9 males and 7 females, mean age 3 days 18·5 hours, range 10 hours to 10 days 21 hours. Eight subjects were tested in each of conditions 5a and 5b.

Procedure.   In condition 5a half the subjects were habituated to a stationary cross, half to a stationary triangle. The two post-criterion trials were paired presentations of triangle and cross, both translating. In condition 5b half the subjects were habituated to a translating cross, half to a translating triangle, with paired triangle and cross, both stationary, shown on the post-criterion trials.

Results

The results are detailed in Table 4. On the post-criterion trials 13 of the 16 subjects looked more at the novel stimulus (six in condition 5a, seven in 5b), and significant novelty preferences were found both overall, and for each of conditions 5a and 5b.

Summary and general conclusions

Several of the results from these experiments are of interest. The least surprising is the confirmation of movement as a salient stimulus dimension for new-borns. In all of the preferential looking studies (Expt 1) where a rotating or translating stimulus was paired with its stationary representation, the moving stimulus was preferred. A rotation of 90°/s was preferred to 180°/s, which may reflect new-borns' processing limitations, but even the fastest rotation was preferred to a stationary stimulus. The habituation study of Expt 2 suggests that clockwise and anticlockwise directions of rotation may be considered equivalent forms of stimulation for new-borns: whether or not they can distinguish between these directions of rotation is not known.

The main focus of these experiments was to investigate new-borns' extraction of shape information from moving and stationary stimuli, and in particular to see whether, and

Table 4. Habituation trials and novelty preferences, Expt 54

Stimuli[a]		No. of subjects	Mean no. of trials to criterion	Mean total fixation time (s)	Mean per cent novelty preference
Familiar	Novel				
Condition 5a					
Cross S	Triangle T	4	6·25	90·5	66·25
Triangle S	Cross T	4	7·5	106·4	72·5
Average			6·9	98·4	69·4**
Condition 5b					
Cross T	Triangle S	4	11·25	165·0	72·2
Triangle T	Cross S	4	8·0	82·6	71·9
Average			9·6	123·8	72·0***
Overall average			8·25	111·1	70·7****

**t = 3·14; ***t = 4·12; ****t = 5·23; all Ps < 0·01.
[a] S = stationary, T = translating.

under what conditions, such information transfers across dimensions (i.e. from stationary to moving, and vice versa). Analyses of the post-habituation trials of Expt 4 suggest that when a stimulus changes from stationary to rotating, and vice versa, then what is learned from the habituation trials does not readily transfer to the changed stimulus conditions. Perhaps under these conditions the stationary (or moving) stimulus is genuinely perceived as being different from its moving (or stationary) counterpart. Alternatively, it might be the case that the additional novelty value of the post-criterion stimuli prevents a novelty response based on the detection of features common to both habituated and post-criterion 'familiar' stimuli from making its appearance. This experiment leaves open both possible interpretations, and also leaves open the question of whether or not new-borns can respond to orientation *per se* as a stimulus variable.

It is clear, however, that (1) the spatiotemporal changes in pattern between a stationary and moving (whether rotating or translating) stimulus are detected and responded to by new-borns, and (2) they can extract shape information both from stationary and from moving stimuli, and can transfer what is learned both within and between stationary and moving conditions. The conditions under which these learned discriminations become apparent are those in which orientation changes are constant from habituation to post-criterion trials (Expt 3), and in which orientation does not change across conditions (Expt 5).

Although the procedures and stimuli used in the present experiments differ in several respects from those used by Ruff (1982), some of the conclusions are common to both studies. In Ruff's experiments, 6-month-old infants showed no significant differentiation of novel and familiar stimuli following continuous rotational transformation of the familiarized stimulus, but translatory movement *was* effective in helping the infants to recognize the stimulus object. The similarities between Ruff's results and ours offer support to the suggestion that the development of at least *some* types of perceptual ability may be primarily quantitative rather than qualitative (Antell & Keating, 1983).

Many current theories of perceptual development emphasize infants' detection of stimulus invariants across a variety of spatiotemporal changes (e.g. Gibson & Spelke, 1983). Bower's claim that infants under 20 weeks cannot detect the form properties of moving objects has been shown to be unfounded. Certainly, new-borns can perceive a perceptual similarity between a stimulus when it is stationary and when it is in motion. These results do not mean, of course, that new-borns perceive the moving and stationary stimuli as the *same* stimulus, but it can nevertheless be concluded that new-borns have the perceptual potential for object identity constancy across stimulus changes from stationary to moving and vice versa.

Acknowledgements

The research was supported by grant nos. C00230028 and C00232114 to the first author from the Economic and Social Research Council. We are indebted to the staff of the Maternity Ward, Royal Devon and Exeter Hospital, Heavitree, Exeter, and to all the subjects' mothers for their cooperation and assistance.

References

Antell, S. A. & Keating, D. P. (1983). Perception of numerical invariance in neonates. *Child Development*, **54**, 695–701.

Aronson, E. & Tronick, E. (1971). Perceptual capacities in early infancy. In J. Eliot (ed.), *Human Development and Cognitive Processes*. London: Holt, Rinehart & Winston.

Ashton, R. (1973). The state variable in neonatal research: A review. *Merrill-Palmer Quarterly of Behavior and Development*, **19**, 3–20.

Aslin, R. N. (1981). Development of smooth pursuit in human infants. In D. F. Fisher, R. A. Monty & J. W. Senders (eds), *Eye Movements: Cognition and Visual Perception*. Hillsdale, NJ: Erlbaum.

Bower, T. G. R. (1971). The object in the world of the infant. *Scientific American*, **225**, 30–38.

Bower, T. G. R. (1974). *Development in Infancy*. San Francisco, CA: Freeman.

Bower, T. G. R., Broughton, J. & Moore, M. K. (1971). Development of the object concept as manifested in changes in the tracking behavior of infants between 7 and 20 weeks of age. *Journal of Experimental Child Psychology*, **11**, 182–193.

Bower, T. G. R. & Paterson, J. G. (1973). The separation of place, movement, and object in the world of the infant. *Journal of Experimental Child Psychology*, **15**, 161–168.

Bronson, G. (1974). The postnatal growth of visual capacity. *Child Development*, **45**, 873–890.

Bronson, G. (1982). *The Scanning Patterns of Human Infants*. Norwood, NJ: Ablex.

Burnham, D. K. & Day, R. H. (1979). Detection of color in rotating objects by infants and its generalisation over changes in velocity. *Journal of Experimental Child Psychology*, **28**, 191–204.

Carpenter, G. C. (1974). Visual regard of moving and stationary faces in early infancy. *Merrill-Palmer Quarterly of Behavior and Development*, **20**, 181–194.

Fantz, R. L. & Nevis, S. (1967). Pattern preferences and perceptual cognitive development in early infancy. *Merrill-Palmer Quarterly of Behavior and Development*, **13**, 77–108.

Gibson, E. J. & Spelke, E. S. (1983). The development of perception. In J. H. Flavell & E. M. Markman (eds), *Handbook of Child Psychology*, vol. 3, *Cognitive Development*. New York: Wiley.

Hartlep, K. L. & Forsyth, G. A. (1977). Infants' discrimination of moving and stationary objects. *Perceptual and Motor Skills*, **45**, 27–33.

Horowitz, F. D., Paden, L., Bhana, K. & Self, P. (1972). An infant-control procedure for studying infant visual fixations. *Developmental Psychology*, **7**, 90.

Maurer, D. & Lewis, T. L. (1979). A physiological explanation of infants' early visual development. *Canadian Journal of Psychology*, **33**, 232–252.

McKenzie, B. A. & Day, R. H. (1976). Infants' attention to stationary and moving objects at different distances. *Australian Journal of Psychology*, **28**, 45–51.

Ruff, H. A. (1982). Effect of object movement on infants' detection of object structure. *Developmental Psychology*, **18**, 462–472.

Slater, A., Morison, V. & Rose, D. (1982). Visual memory at birth. *British Journal of Psychology*, **73**, 519–525.

Slater, A., Morison, V. & Rose, D. (1983a). Perception of shape by the new-born baby. *British Journal of Developmental Psychology*, **1**, 135–142.

Slater, A., Morison, V. & Rose, D. (1983b). Locus of habituation in the human newborn. *Perception*, **12**, 593–598.

Slater, A., Morison, V. & Rose, D. (1984a). Habituation in the newborn. *Infant Behavior and Development*, **7**, 183–200.

Slater, A., Rose, D. & Morison, V. (1984b). New-born infants' perception of similarities and differences between two- and three-dimensional stimuli. *British Journal of Developmental Psychology*, **2**, 287–294.

Tronick, E. (1972). Stimulus control and the growth of the infant's effective visual field. *Perception and Psychophysics*, **11**, 373–376.

Volkmann, F. C. & Dobson, M. V. (1976). Infant responses of ocular fixation to moving visual stimuli. *Journal of Experimental Child Psychology*, **22**, 86–99.

Werner, J.S. & Perlmutter, M. (1979). Development of visual memory in infants. *Advances in Child Development and Behavior*, **14**, 1–56.

Wilcox, B.M. & Clayton, F. L. (1968). Infant visual fixation on motion pictures of the human face. *Journal of Experimental Child Psychology*, **6**, 22–32.

Requests for reprints should be addressed to Alan Slater, Department of Psychology, Washington Singer Laboratories, University of Exeter, Exeter EX4 4QG, UK.

V. Morison and C. Town are also at the above address.

D. Rose is now at the Psychology Department, Plymouth Polytechnic, Devon.

British Journal of Developmental Psychology (1985), **3**, 221–228   *Printed in Great Britain*

Aesthetic perception of faces during infancy*

Curtis A. Samuels and **Richard Ewy**

This study explores the visual preferences of young infants for faces that differ with respect to their perceived attractiveness, as evaluated by adult raters. Black-and-white slides were presented to infants in 12 paired comparisons. Both 3-month-old ($n = 26$) and 6-month-old ($n = 35$) infants looked longer at the faces rated attractive. Pairs were constructed so that members of each pair were as similar as possible in gross physical appearance, differing only in rated attractiveness. The implications of an aesthetic sensitivity in such young infants are briefly explored.

It has been said that 'beauty is in the eye of the beholder'. All of us have accumulated our personal evidence that substantiates the validity of this point. Yet the question that Plato grappled with still persists: is there a universal standard for aesthetic evaluation?

The problem of aesthetic appreciation is not new to experimental psychology. Valentine (1913) discussed various components to consider in a formal analysis including: colour, form, balance and symmetry, meaning, association and memory. However, the developmental question did not occur to him. It is of interest to establish whether sensitivity to aesthetics can be demonstrated in early infancy.

The question explored in this report is when might such an aesthetic sensitivity emerge in development? The possibility of an innate aesthetic sensibility should not be discarded without due consideration. Fantz (1963) demonstrated that young infants have visual preferences at less than one week of age. His pioneering work (Fantz, 1958, 1963; Fantz, Ordy & Udelf, 1962; Fantz, Fagan & Miranda, 1975) showed that infants (a) display greater visual interest in patterns than in plain colours, (b) differentiate among patterns of similar complexity, (c) prefer curved forms to linear ones, (d) prefer symmetrical to asymmetrical patterns, and (e) show particular interest in a pattern similar to a human face.

Leaving aside for the moment the innateness question, when, if at all, during infancy do aesthetic considerations play a role in allocation of attention? It has been shown that differential attention of 4-month-old infants to various colours parallels the ratings of pleasantness of those same colours by adults (Bornstein, 1975).

Work by Barrera & Maurer has shown that 3-month-old infants discriminate pictures of their mothers from strangers (Barrera & Maurer, 1981b), and that 3-month-olds discriminate strangers who look rather different physiognomically, as well as strangers who look similar to each other (Barrera & Maurer, 1981a). The subtle facial discriminations required of the infants in this latter case illustrate the sensitivity to facial detail of the 3-month-old. This interest in and sensitivity to faces make them excellent candidates to serve as stimuli in this test of the infants' perception of aesthetic attractiveness.

Various authors have conducted studies employing faces in diverse forms of presentation including normal facial photographs, schematic faces, scrambled faces, cyclops and featureless 'faces'. While these authors did not consider their stimuli to vary on any

---
*Portions of this paper were presented at the Biennial Meeting of the Society for Research in Child Development, April 1985, Toronto, Canada.

aesthetic dimension, we suggest that an aesthetic component may have been present in determining infants' attention distribution.

Hershenson (1965) showed 20 new-born infants the face of Joan Crawford in normal presentation and in a distorted fashion (with the outline of the head and hair retained, but with the features scrambled). He found no differential attention to these stimuli. Presumably, the 'scrambled' face was aesthetically less attractive than the normal presentation (according to criteria of form, balance, symmetry, association or memory). Thus, the neonates in his study of 'figural organization' did not show an adult-like aesthetic preference pattern. It may be that aesthetics was confounded with some other factor in this work, such as novelty; or perhaps the neonates were not attending to the features inside the hair/head outline, as work by Bergman *et al.* (1971), Maurer & Salapatek (1976) and Hainline (1978) indicates. If new-borns look mostly to the outer edges of objects, they might not even have noticed the scrambled vs. normal facial differences. However, a recent study by Maurer (1983) indicates that new-borns and 1-month-old infants will look at the internal features of a schematic face. She additionally reports that new-borns fixated the internal features of the schematic face more than an internal square within a frame. These results lead to the hypothesis that organizational properties of the face (aesthetic attractiveness included) may not be as salient for very young infants as are stimulus parameters such as complexity and contrast information.

Several authors have studied older infants employing various face and face-like stimuli. Kagan *et al.* (1966) found that 4-month-old infants preferred a face-like stimulus to a scrambled (features rearranged) face stimulus. The index for this preference was their smiling. Haaf & Bell (1967) with 4-month-olds and Haaf (1977) with $3\frac{1}{2}$- and 5-month-olds found similar preferences for a schematic facial presentation over a scrambled face; in these studies he employed visual fixation time as the dependent measure. It was observed that the degree of 'faceness' and stimulus complexity was a determining factor for the infants' visual behaviour. However, Haaf (1974) with 5- and 10-week-olds found no evidence for preferences based on a facial resemblance dimension. Rather, he found a significant complexity component in the responses for both groups. Again, it seems that younger infants are more aware of stimulus parameters like complexity and contrast, while only infants older than 2 or 3 months are alert to faceness and organizational properties.

Wilcox (1969), with 4-, 10- and 16-week-old infants, explored the visual preferences for various degrees of complexity and 'faceness'. Her scrambled face differed from the previously employed scrambled face stimuli by rearranging the facial features into a non-face-like configuration symmetrical about the vertical axis. She concluded that the visual preferences were controlled more strongly by complexity and perhaps contrast than by the degree of resemblance to a human face. Similarly, Koopman & Ames (1968) failed to find discrimination of featural configuration with $2\frac{1}{2}$-month-old infants.

Lewis (1969) conducted a developmental study of infants' responses to facial and face-like stimuli. He tested infants of 12, 24, 36 and 57 weeks of age, showing them four facial arrays: a scrambled schematic, a normal schematic, a cyclops photo and a normal photo. Lewis found stimulus effects only at 3 and 6 months of age. The 3-month-olds preferred the more realistic faces—the photographs to the line drawings. The 6-month-olds preferred the faces with all their features normally positioned to the faces with missing or distorted features (as tended the 9-month-olds, albeit not significantly).

Our study was designed to explore the visual preferences of young infants presented with two faces differing in 'facial attractiveness'. Two age groups, 3 months and 6 months, viewed two photos simultaneously, an attractive face and a similar gender/size/race face judged less attractive by adult raters. It was expected that the group of faces aesthetically preferred by adults would similarly be preferred by the 6-month-old infants to the less attractive stimulus pair. Previous research showed that younger infants tended to be somewhat insensitive to more subtle organizational qualities within the face. We therefore expected no differentiation between the more and less attractive faces by the 3-month-old infants.

Method

The experiment was conducted in our laboratory at the Institute of Human Development in Berkeley, California. A forced-choice paired comparison situation was employed using black-and-white slides of faces. The dependent measure was the amount of looking by the infants to the left or the right presentation screen.

Subjects

The sample consisted of 61 infants: 3-month-old boys ($n = 15$), 6-month-old boys ($n = 19$), 3-month-old girls ($n = 11$), and 6-month-old girls ($n = 16$). The names of 91 infants were obtained from local birth record lists and babies were volunteered by their parents to come into our laboratory. They all met screening criteria of normal deliveries, weighed between 2500 and 4300 grams at birth, and had no obvious health problems. Thirty infants failed to complete the viewing task, 14 due to fussiness, and the data from 16 were discarded due to a side bias in their viewing. A side bias was determined by the *a priori* criteria of the infant viewing exclusively to one side on at least half of the trials, or by attending more to either side on all 12 test trials in the viewing session. However, there was a differential drop-out rate for the infants at the two ages—24 3-month-olds and six 6-month-olds. This was probably due to the difficulty parents had in determining their infants' schedules, with respect to when baby would be well fed and well rested and in a mood conducive to participation in the study.

Stimuli

Thirteen pairs of slides were employed as stimuli and were rear-projected on to two screens. The first slide pair (pair 0) was a 'warm-up' pair, showing identical colour photos of a human hand. The remaining 12 pairs of slides were the experimental stimuli. These were black-and-white slide photographs of faces, six pairs of male adult faces, and six pairs of female adult faces. In one stimulus pair for each gender (pairs 2 and 9) the models wore eyeglasses). Pairs were constructed to contain one face that was considered by a panel of 250 adult raters as attractive and one face that was unattractive, which constituted our aesthetic manipulation. Otherwise, each pair was matched as closely as possible on factors such as hair colour and style, clothing, gaze direction, size of the face, contrast and brightness, angle of facial presentation and facial expression. All of the faces in this study were equally real and complex, in that they were photos of actual faces; and in general they were equally unfamiliar, in that they were all novel faces for each infant. However, in pair 2 we failed to match hair colour (the 'attractive' face had lighter hair), and in pair 6 we failed to match for emotional expression (the attractive face was smiling while the 'unattractive' face was surprised with a wild look in the eyes).

The panel of raters had no difficulty in reaching consensus about the attractiveness of the facial stimuli; 100 stimuli were presented sequentially and evaluated on a simple three-point rating scale (less than average/average/ better than average attractiveness), and their mean correlation was 0.88. Only stimuli with an inter-rater correlation above 0.95 were selected for use in the study. The facial stimuli were obtained from a college yearbook, members of an early 1970s graduating class from a large East coast American university.

Procedure

Mothers brought their infants into a laboratory room and placed them in an infant seat. Subjects were placed in front of a three-partition rear projection apparatus at a viewing distance of 48 cm. Each partition was angled so that when the infants turned to look at a picture presented either to the left or right, the viewing screen was perpendicular to their line of sight. Two Kodak carousel projectors presented the slide stimuli in a synchronous fashion. Slide presentation onset and offset was controlled by the laboratory computer such that the presentation times for each slide pair was exactly 10 s. Length of the inter-trial interval was determined by the infants' own visual behaviour. The infant was required to fixate centrally between the two screens for at least 1·5 s before the next pair was presented; this was encouraged by the use of a blinking red central fixation light, accompanied by a gently beeping tone.

The mother withdrew from the infant's visual field and the experimenter went to the back of the rear projection apparatus to observe the baby's visual fixations through a small, centrally located peephole. The observer could not see the position of the aesthetically attractive slide within each pair, or which pair was being seen by the infant. The observer was, however, aware of which of the two stimulus arrangements the infants were viewing, as he placed the carousel slide trays on to the projectors for the arrangement manipulation, but he did not know the order of the slides.

The left and right visual fixations of the infants were monitored by the observer and stored by the laboratory computer for analysis. This observation method has been employed in our own and other laboratories, and yields inter-observer reliability coefficients in our laboratory of 0·90–0·97 (Fagan, 1972; Samuels, 1985); in this experiment, inter-observer agreement was not directly evaluated. Half of the infants saw the pairs of slides in arrangement A, and half of the sample saw the slides in arrangement B, which was left–right reversed, to counterbalance for any possible side-effects. The experimental sessions lasted 4–7 minutes.*

Results

An attractiveness (2) × age (2) × infants' gender (2) × stimulus order (2) repeated measures analysis of variance was computed with seconds of fixation to the visual stimuli as the dependent variable. (A second analysis was done in which the data were transformed to proportional looking times for each stimulus pair for each infant. Because the results of this analysis were nearly identical to those reported below based on absolute looking times they are not additionally reported.) Surprisingly, there was no main effect for age, nor was there an effect for gender, nor for the control variable of stimulus order. However, there was a large main effect for attractiveness of the facial stimuli ($F = 277 \cdot 33$, d.f. $= 1,57$, $P < 0 \cdot 0001$). There were no interactions of age, gender or arrangement with the aesthetic attractiveness manipulation.

To be certain that neither age group was primarily responsible for generating the significant effects of stimulus attractiveness, separate 2×2 ANOVAs were conducted (attractiveness × infant's gender) on the 3-month-old sample and on the 6-month-old sample. Both age groups showed a significant preference for the more attractive stimulus faces (3-month-olds: $F = 91 \cdot 55$, d.f. $= 1,24$, $P < 0 \cdot 0001$; 6-month-olds: $F = 221 \cdot 97$, d.f. $= 1,33$, $P < 0 \cdot 0001$).

A separate ANOVA was performed to examine the relationship between infant's gender and the gender of the stimulus face. There was no overall effect for sex of the stimulus face. However, there was a significant interaction of infant's gender with gender of the stimulus face ($F = 5 \cdot 32$, d.f. $= 1,57$, $P < 0 \cdot 05$). The male infants preferred to attend to the female stimulus faces, but the female babies looked equally to both male and female stimulus faces.

Our analysis of the paired comparisons was accomplished through individual planned comparison ANOVAs [attractiveness (2) × age(2) × infant's gender (2)] for each stimulus pair. These results are summarized in Table 1, showing the mean fixation times in seconds and the F value for each pair of the slide stimuli.

It can be seen from Table 1 that 11 of the 12 pairs of faces (i.e. pairs 1–12; pair 0 is the control pair) produced differential fixation beyond the $0 \cdot 001$ probability level. In every case, the direction of effect was for the infants to favour the slide considered aesthetically attractive by the panel of adult raters. In all 12 of the stimulus pairs the attractive pair received more visual attention than the unattractive pair. The consistency of the finding and the magnitude of effect are surprisingly robust.

In pair 0 (the control slides which served as a warm-up pair to orient the infants to the paired comparison procedure) there was no attentional preference for either of the identical slides, as expected. For the facial stimuli, the only pair where a significant preference for the 'attractive' stimulus face was *not* found was pair 6. It is interesting that this was the particular pair where we had failed to match the stimuli on the portrayed emotional expression. Specifically, the 'attractive' face showed a smiling female, while its 'unattractive' counterpart depicted a woman with a surprised (almost frightened) look on her face. This wide-eyed surprised face contained an unusual degree of 'animation', and perhaps this factor contributed to the distribution of the infants' attention.

---

*This study was part of a larger procedure in which a prior set of slides in paired comparison was presented to the infants. In advance of the attractive/unattractive paired faces, the infants saw 11 paired photographs from Eckman & Friesen's (1978) Facial Action Coding System's action unit photographs. All of our sample, then, first saw 11 pairs of black-and-white slides of a male model (Eckman) illustrating various emotional expressions. Following this, the infants viewed the slides that have been described above. The duration of the entire procedure was about 6–7 minutes.

Table 1. Mean attention time (s) to the face pairs and significance level

Pair number	Attractive	Unattractive	*F* value	Probability
0 Hands	3·21	3·03	0·04	0·849
1 Female	4·30	1·81	25·61	0·000
2 Male	4·10	2·08	19·98	0·000
3 Male	4·30	2·25	23·13	0·000
4 Female	4·70	1·61	51·09	0·000
5 Male	4·37	1·51	66·16	0·000
6 Female	3·28	2·97	0·16	0·694
7 Male	4·81	1·69	52·85	0·000
8 Female	3·81	1·82	24·97	0·000
9 Female	3·91	1·89	17·82	0·000
10 Male	4·42	1·30	78·99	0·000
11 Male	4·56	0·92	77·77	0·000
12 Female	4·15	1·45	34·64	0·000

Several of the pairs had significant interactions in addition to the main effect. Pair 1 had an interaction of infant's gender with attractiveness ($F=7·40$, d.f. $= 1,57$, $P<0·01$), with the males showing a stronger preference for the attractive female stimulus than the female babies. Pair 3 evidenced an aesthetics × age interaction ($F=5·55$, d.f. $= 1,57$, $P<0·05$); both the 3- and 6-month-olds preferred the attractive face, with the younger babies showing a more pronounced effect. In pair 6 there was a three-way aesthetics × infant's gender × age interaction ($F=4·02$, d.f. $= 1,57$, $P<0·05$) which showed that the 3-month-old male babies strongly preferred the attractive stimulus and the 6-month-old female babies slightly preferred the attractive face; the 6-month-old males and the 3-month-old females looked to the two stimuli approximately equally. Finally, pair 10 showed an attractiveness × gender interaction ($F=5·07$, d.f. $= 1,57$, $P<0·05$), as well as a three-way attractiveness × infant's gender × age interaction ($F=4·74$, d.f. $= 1,57$, $P<0·05$) with both the males and females having the same directional preference for the attractive slide but the females showing an even stronger preference, especially at 3 months of age. Given the numerous possible two-way and three-way interactions that could have been obtained (but were not), and since these interactions fail to paint a unified picture that sheds more light on the phenomenon under study, we consider these few interactions to be 'noise' rather than meaningful or systematic results.

To test an alternative explanation for our results, an informal analysis of the slides' informational content was carried out using a procedure recommended by Banks (1984) which roughly estimates the energy or contrast in low spatial frequencies (LSF) contained in each slide picture. Three persons knowledgeable about infant perceptual abilities viewed the slide pairs which were sufficiently out of focus so that the facial attractiveness was not discernable. The stimuli were de-focused so that internal featural detail was very unclear; the direction of eye-gaze or the extent of mouth opening was not visible to the adult raters. Predictions of infants' preferences (strong left, mild left, equal, mild right, strong right) were made on the basis of differences in visible detail and contrast information. The results of the three raters were averaged to predict pairwise preferences based on the LSF model. Such an informal analysis falls far short of the technical rigour employed by Banks and his associates with their LSF method (Banks & Salapatek, 1981), but still allows prediction of infants' preferences if their preferences are based solely on the amount of contrast present in gross facial features.

Infants' preferences were better predicted by the aesthetic preference model (12 of 12 mean attention times favoured the attractive stimulus) than by the low spatial frequency model (8 of 12 mean attention times favoured the stimulus richer in information). Such an informal analysis is not intended to be a definitive test of the two models; nonetheless, we find the results interesting.

Discussion

The results of this study indicate that infants, even at 3 and 6 months of age, have visual preferences for attractive faces over unattractive faces that correspond to adults' judgements of attractiveness. This leads to speculation that infants have an underlying aesthetic sense similar to an adult aesthetic evaluation of faces. Our expectation at the outset of the study was that the 6-month-old infants might evidence such aesthetic preferences, but that the 3-month-old infants would not. It was thought that the 3-month-olds' preferences would be governed more by gross physical characteristics of the stimulus faces than by subtle aesthetic differences, and would therefore randomly attend to these facial stimuli.

The robustness of the effect, both for the 6- and the 3-month-olds, suggests the possibility that such aesthetic preferences for attractive faces over unattractive ones derive from a disposition present very early in life. While it is possible that young babies are conditioned to prefer the attractive faces, this is not very likely to be a workable explanation for these data. Selective reinforcement by the parents for attending to aesthetically appealing faces is probably not a common practice. However, the possibility exists that an internal reinforcement could be strengthening an already extant aesthetic disposition; intrinsic gratification from attending to beautiful or pleasing events would reinforce such attentional allocation. Additionally, the 12 stimulus pairs were selected to represent a wide range of appearance, so similarity of the individual pairs to parents' faces could not be an important confounding factor.

It might be asked why infants would show a preference for faces that are attractive or whether there is some value in such a sensitivity. We would recast these questions into whether there is an *affordance* yielded by perception of the aesthetic. J. J. Gibson's (1977, 1979) theory of perception introduced the concept of affordances—information for behaviour that is of some potential utility to an animal—'The affordances of the environment are what it "offers" the animal, what it "provides" or "furnishes", either for good or ill' (1979, p. 127). E. J. Gibson (1982) extended the theory in saying that 'affordances of things and events can be much more complicated, especially when we enter the realm of social events and what other people afford' (p. 77). An affordance may therefore be a rather abstract percept not limited to physical objects but existing also in the realm of functional social cognition. Social behaviour in part depends on the affordances offered by social objects. In philosophy, the aesthetic and the functional are often thought to represent opposites. We would prefer to think of them as orthogonal dimensions. However, an aesthetic perception for human faces seems to offer no particular affordance, i.e. to serve no functional end (at least not an obvious one). Caregivers, either attractive or unattractive facially, could be equally loving in their child-rearing habits; no research of which we are aware indicates any behavioural differences for attractive or unattractive adults in their treatment of infants. If, as we speculate, an aesthetic preference affords nothing, this only makes more puzzling the results obtained in this study.

While we know that adults can judge infants' physical attractiveness (Hildebrandt, 1983), so too do infants evaluate adult faces on an aesthetic dimension; it seems this evaluative process is a reciprocal one. However, on what basis do these infants prefer the more attractive faces? Many possibilities exist, including symmetry of the face, size of the eyes or mouth, shape of the facial features, or perhaps a similarity to the modal 'baby face' by the adult faces may have led to the infants' differential attention. Hildebrandt & Fitzgerald

(1979) and Maier *et al.* (1984) have shown that adults rate as more attractive babies whose faces depict greater 'babyishness', with large foreheads and eyes, small nose and lips, and fat cheeks, all on a roundish face. We have not analysed our experimental stimuli according to these properties of babyishness; it is possible that this type of facial configuration is also more attractive for infant subjects.

Alternatively, the role of symmetry (particularly vertical symmetry) in determining the infant's preferences for the various facial stimuli has not been systematically assessed in our study. Work by Bornstein *et al.* (1981) and Fisher *et al.* (1981) has shown that 4-month-old infants discriminate vertically symmetrical patterns from asymmetrical or horizontally symmetrical stimuli and process the vertically symmetrical patterns more efficiently. While cursory inspection of our stimuli did not reveal any major asymmetrically distributed faces (along the vertical axis), more precise examination of this factor may reveal a source for the preferences we have obtained. These questions currently remain unanswered.

Future research is needed to detail the extent of an aesthetic sensitivity in young infants. Faces were chosen in this study to maximize interest in the experimental stimuli since it has been repeatedly noticed that infants show interest in facial stimuli (e.g. Spitz & Wolf, 1946; Ambrose, 1961). Will an aesthetic preference by infants generalize to other domains than human faces? Does their aesthetic sensitivity extend to works of fine art? Will moving pictures show that infants prefer graceful motion to awkward motions? Do infants show their aesthetic preferences based on visual appeal or on more complex compositional qualities? Is there any innate aesthetic component in the attentional allocation of very young infants? In what manner might preferences during infancy contribute to the later development of an aesthetic sensitivity in adulthood? To what extent does a cultural component dictate aesthetic preferences for faces or other stimuli? These questions remain open for future empirical research.

The data presented here indicate that young infants, at both 3 months and 6 months of age, prefer to attend to faces which are seen as attractive by adult raters than to matched faces rated as unattractive. In light of this evidence, it seems likely that the beginnings of an aesthetic sensibility appear even during early infancy.

Acknowledgements

This research was supported by grant no. T32-HB07181 to the first author from NICHHD. Thanks are extended to John S. Watson for his helpful advice and criticism, and to an anonymous reviewer whose comments strengthened the presentation of these results.

References

Ambrose, J. A. (1961). The development of the smiling response in early infancy. In B. M. Foss (ed.), *Determinants of Infant Behavior*, vol. 2. New York: Wiley.
Banks, M. (1984). Personal communication.
Banks, M. S. & Salapatek, P. (1981). Infant pattern vision: A new approach based on the contrast sensitivity function. *Journal of Experimental Child Psychology*, **31**, 1–45.
Barrera, M. E. & Maurer, D. (1981*a*). Discrimination of strangers by three-month-old infants. *Child Development*, **52**, 558–563.
Barrera, M. E. & Maurer, D. (1981*b*). Recognition of the mother's photographed face by three-month-old infants. *Child Development*, **52**, 714–716.
Bergman, T., Haith, M. & Mann, L. (1971). Development of eye contact and face scanning in infants. Paper presented at the meeting of the Society for Research in Child Development, Minneapolis, April.
Bornstein, M. H. (1975). Qualities of color vision in infancy. *Journal of Experimental Child Psychology*, **19**, 401–419.
Bornstein, M. H., Ferdinandsen, K. & Gross, C. G. (1981). Perception of symmetry in infancy. *Developmental Psychology*, **17**, 82–86.
Fagan, J. F. (1972). Infants' recognition memory for faces. *Journal of Experimental Child Psychology*, **14**, 453–476.
Fantz, R. L. (1958). Pattern vision in young infants. *The Psychological Record*, **8**, 43–47.

Fantz, R. L. (1963). Pattern vision in newborn infants. *Science*, **140**, 296–297.

Fantz, R. L. Fagan, J. F., III & Miranda, S. B. (1975). Early visual selectivity as a function of pattern variables, previous exposure, age from birth and conception, and expected cognitive deficit. In L. B. Cohen & P. Salapatek (eds), *Infant Perception*, vol. 1. New York: Academic Press.

Fantz, R. L., Ordy, J. M. & Udelf, M. S. (1962). Maturation of pattern vision in infants during the first six months. *Journal of Comparative and Physiological Psychology*, **55**, 907–917.

Fisher, C. B., Ferdinandsen, K. & Bornstein, M. H. (1981). The role of symmetry in infant form discrimination. *Child Development*, **52**, 457–462.

Gibson, E. J. (1982). The concept of affordances in development: The renaissance of functionalism. In W. A. Collins (ed.), *The Concept of Development. Minnesota Symposium on Child Psychology*, vol. 15. Hillsdale, NJ: Erlbaum.

Gibson, J. J. (1977). The theory of affordances. In R. Shaw & J. Bransford (eds), *Handbook of Perception*, vol. 1. New York: Academic Press.

Gibson, J. J. (1979). *The Ecological Approach to Visual Perception*. Boston, MA: Houghton-Mifflin.

Haaf, R. A. (1974). Complexity and facial resemblance as determinants of response to facelike stimuli by 5- and 10-week-old infants. *Journal of Experimental Child Psychology*, **18**, 480–487.

Haaf, R. A. (1977). Visual response to complex facelike patterns by 15- and 20-week-old infants. *Developmental Psychology*, **13**, 77–78.

Haaf, R. A. & Bell, R. Q. (1967). A facial dimension in visual discrimination by human infants. *Child Development*, **38**, 893–899.

Hainline, L. (1978). Developmental changes in visual scanning of face and nonface patterns by infants. *Journal of Experimental Child Psychology*, **25**, 90–115.

Hershenson, M. (1965). Visual discrimination in the human newborn. *Dissertation Abstracts*, **26**, 1793.

Hildebrandt, K. A. (1983). Effect of facial expression variations on ratings of infants' physical attractiveness. *Developmental Psychology*, **19**, 414–417.

Hildebrandt, K. A. & Fitzgerald, H. E. (1979). Facial featural determinants of infant attractiveness. *Infant Behavior and Development*, **2**, 329–339.

Kagan, J., Henker, B., Hen-Tov, A., Levine, J. & Lewis, M. (1966). Infants' differential reactions to familiar and distorted faces. *Child Development*, **37**, 519–532.

Koopman, P. R. & Ames, E. W. (1968). Infants' preferences for facial arrangements: A failure to replicate. *Child Development*, **39**, 481–487.

Lewis, M. (1969). Infants' responses to facial stimuli during the first year of life. *Developmental Psychology*, **1**, 75–86.

Maier, R. A., Holmes, D. L., Slaymaker, F. L. & Reich, J. N. (1984). The perceived attractiveness of preterm infants. *Infant Behavior and Development*, **7**, 403–414.

Maurer, D. (1983). The scanning of compound figures by young infants. *Journal of Experimental Child Psychology*, **35**, 437–448.

Maurer, D. & Salapatek, P. (1976). Developmental changes in the scanning of faces by young infants. *Child Development*, **47**, 523–527.

Samuels, C. A. (1985). Attention to eye contact opportunity and facial motion by three-month-old infants. *Journal of Experimental Child Psychology*.

Spitz, R. A. & Wolf, K. M. (1946). The smiling response: A contribution to the ontogenesis of social relations. *Genetic Psychology Monographs*, **34**, 57–125.

Valentine, C. W. (1913). *An Introduction to the Experimental Psychology of Beauty*. London: T. C. & E. C. Jack/ Dodge Publishing Co.

Wilcox, B. M. (1969). Visual preferences of human infants for representations of the human face. *Journal of Experimental Child Psychology*, **7**, 10–20.

Wolff, P. (1961). Observations on the early development of smiling. In B. M. Foss (ed.), *Determinants of Infant Behaviour*, vol. 2. London: Methuen.

Requests for reprints should be sent to Curtis Samuels or Richard Ewy, Department of Psychology, University of California, Berkeley, CA 94720, USA.

British Journal of Developmental Psychology (1985), **3**, 229–242   *Printed in Great Britain*

Corneal reflection eye-movement recording as a measure of infant pattern perception: What do we really know?

Louise Hainline and Elizabeth Lemerise

Infra-red corneal reflection techniques have been used for a number of years to assess infant pattern perception. The existing studies using this method have been interpreted as supporting the existence of a developmental trend in pattern scanning from narrow to more extensive pattern scanning over the first few months of life; these changes have been attributed to the development of cortical functioning. We discuss the possible sources of error in the use of these techniques with infants, and critically evaluate the conclusions that have been drawn from the existing studies. In addition to technical limitations in the early corneal reflection work, failure to take account of the infant's state of alertness may have caused younger infants to seem visually less capable than they really are. Based on this review of the existing literature and on a reanalysis of our data on scanning in early infancy (Hainline & Lemerise, 1982), we conclude that, at present, there are few data that unequivocally support the claimed developmental change in scanning extensiveness in early infancy.

Introduction

The past 20–30 years have been extremely productive in the area of research on infancy. In part, this is due to increasingly sophisticated research methods made possible by improved technology. One of these methods is corneal reflection photography, a technique for specifying with some precision the eye's point of regard in space. Initially applied to human infants in the pioneering research of Kessen, Salapatek and Haith (Salapatek & Kessen, 1966, 1973; Haith, 1969), the technique offered graphic evidence that human infants attend selectively to different parts of visual stimuli and actively scan their environments, presumably processing visual information as they do so.

These early studies were interpreted as indicating that, while young infants actively scanned visual stimuli, the precise pattern of their scanning was under the control of, or even captured by, the stimulus. Neonates (Salapatek & Kessen, 1966; Kessen *et al.*, 1972) and infants under 2 months of age (Salapatek, 1969, 1975) were described as being particularly attracted by high contrast edges, repeatedly crossing over them with their eye movements and keeping their fixations close to these features. For simple geometric forms such as large triangles, neonates (Salapatek & Kessen, 1966; Nelson & Kessen, 1969) and infants under 2 months (Salapatek, 1969, 1975) failed to scan the entire figure, instead concentrating their scans on a single region of high contrast contour. Despite the fact that there were also data showing that neonates exhibited whole figure scanning (Salapatek & Kessen, 1973) and that modifying the size of the figure changed the pattern of scanning (Salapatek, 1967, 1968), the early results were interpreted to mean that under 2 months of age infants' reduced extensiveness of scanning reflected a difference in the processing of pattern information because of neural immaturities in the central visual system, particularly the visual cortex (Bronson, 1974; Salapatek, 1975). These scanning data were seen as consistent with data on visual discrimination and memory (e.g. Cohen & Gelber, 1975) that showed no evidence of discrimination and memory prior to 2 months. After 2 months the pattern of scanning was claimed to change to a more extensive scan of an entire figure (Salapatek, 1969, 1975); at the same time infants showed evidence of discrimination and memory. This change was attributed to maturation of central, visual pattern-encoding mechanisms; thus, these early studies fostered the belief that studies of infant scanning could provide relatively direct information about the status of neurological development in the visual system. An important recent review of the literature on infant pattern perception (Banks & Salapatek, 1983) concluded that the bulk of the available evidence [primarily the data of Salapatek (1969) reanalysed in Salapatek (1975), and Leahy (1976)] supports the existence of a developmental trend in scanning extensiveness over the first three months.

There are, however, two independent lines of research that cast doubt on the impression of the infant under 2 months as only reflexively responsive or 'subcortical'. First, work on habituation in neonates has demonstrated that even new-borns are capable of visual discrimination and memory (e.g. Slater *et al.*, 1982, 1983*a*, *b*, 1984, and this issue). New-borns have shown evidence of discrimination and memory when a variant of the usual fixed trials habituation procedure is used. New-born infants in Slater *et al.*'s studies actively sampled both members of a pair of simultaneously presented stimuli; they did not look at only one stimulus as had been previously claimed (Haith, 1980). In these studies, infant control procedures were used and careful attention was paid to behavioural state; for testing, babies were seated upright without pacifiers.

As a second line of evidence, there are scanning data from infants which show stimulus-appropriate scanning with no age differences from 1 to 3 months of age (Hainline & Lemerise, 1982). We collected data from infants between 1 and 3 months with a method of recording eye movements that offered a number of improvements over the techniques previously used with infants (the differences in technique are discussed below). Infants viewed simple geometric forms (circles, squares and triangles) that varied in size from 5° to 30°. The results provided no evidence that scanning by infants under 2 months was 'narrowly' confined to a portion of the figure, with increased scanning extensiveness at older ages. Infants of all the ages studied showed great variability in how they scanned all of the geometric figures, sometimes scanning 'narrowly' and sometimes scanning 'extensively'. Although infants' scanning was clearly related to the size of the stimuli, with infants of all ages showing a more thorough scan of smaller than larger figures, this study failed to find the significant age trends in scanning extensiveness that the earlier studies had reported.

In evaluating the data on pattern scanning in older infants, Banks & Salapatek (1983) criticized Hainline & Lemerise's (1982) results, and continued to argue for a developmental change in scanning extensiveness. Since there are very few studies (see Table 1) which have dealt with the scanning of simple forms beyond the new-born period, it is important to evaluate carefully Banks & Salapatek's criticisms of our 1982 study. Their specific criticisms were: (1) that there were problems of measurement and calibration in our application of corneal reflection methods which restricted the validity of our eye-movement data; and (2) that we used an incorrect definition of scanning extensiveness, misreading definitions offered in earlier papers, and thus did the wrong analyses of infant scanning. As a result, Banks & Salapatek claimed that Hainline & Lemerise (1982) were not able to address adequately the issue of the developmental change in scanning extensiveness during the early months of infancy.

In this paper, we re-examine the infant pattern-scanning literature in order to resolve the discrepancies between earlier work and more recent studies. The issue of calibration in measuring scanning extensiveness is examined for all of the studies. In order to answer the criticisms of Banks & Salapatek (1983), further analyses of the Hainline & Lemerise (1982) data are presented. In addition, other possible reasons for the discrepancies are explored, in particular, the role of infant state in scanning.

Sources of error: Corneal reflection methods and the calibration issue

Banks & Salapatek (1983) implied that there are special problems involved with the Hainline & Lemerise (1982) data because the study 'did not calibrate' the infants' eye-movement data. Calibration, of course, involves procedures for bringing recorded measurements of eye position into better correspondence with the true eye position; issues of calibration apply equally to all studies using corneal reflection methods. There are two general classes of measurements that require calibration: dynamic characteristics (e.g. velocity of eye movements) which are primarily instrument-dependent, and spatial characteristics (accuracy of the estimate of where in space the eye is pointed) which depend both on the instrument and on factors that differ from indivdual to individual. To evaluate the issue of the adequacy of the calibration in any particular study, it is necessary to discuss briefly the sources of error in corneal reflection methods as they are used with infants.

Dynamic error. Since information about change in eye position over time is of interest, one must be concerned with the characteristics of the recording instrument that limit the bandwidth of recording (Harris *et al.*, 1984); rate of sampling eye position is a relevant variable in this case. Until recently, the sampling rate of systems recording infant eye movements was so low [1 Hz (e.g. Salapatek & Kessen, 1966; Leahy, 1976) to 4 Hz (e.g. Salapatek, 1975)] that it was impossible to consider eye position as a continuous variable; each 'sample' of eye position, taken at a fixed sample rate, has simply been considered a 'fixation', and the area of the stimulus corresponding to the estimated point of regard has been assumed to be available for visual processing. The validity of the assumption that the eye is 'fixating' up to four times per second (Haith, 1980) appears to be based on an assessment of the frequency of adults' saccades (the rapid eye movements which relocate the eye between fixations) and the duration of adults' fixations. Researchers using a low sampling rate have argued that any samples taken during a saccade can be distinguished from a fixation by blur in the photographic image of the eye, although the validity of this assumption has not been demonstrated in any published work. To some extent, blur depends on the various factors that determine the speed of the imaging device, but it also depends on how rapidly the eye is in fact moving. With the higher sampling rates now available [60 Hz (Aslin, 1981; Hainline, 1981a)], it is possible to isolate actual fixational and saccadic episodes—an important advance since these two types of episode occur asynchronously, not at fixed intervals tied to sample rate.

In our recent studies of infant oculo-motor control (Hainline, 1984; Hainline *et al.*, 1984), we have discovered characteristics of infant eye movements that lead us seriously to question whether methods with slow (1–4 Hz) sampling rates are adequate to determine the location of infants' actual fixations. First, we observe that infant fixations are often (though not always) briefer than those of adults, so that a given sample is less likely to be an actual fixation for an infant compared with an adult. Second, when the infant is looking at relatively uninteresting displays (such as the geometric forms commonly used in the studies at issue here), we find that even infants who appear to be alert and attentive make saccades that are slower than those made to more interesting stimuli; the fact that infant saccades may, in some cases, have lower velocities reduces the likelihood that the moving eye will appear to be blurred on a given sample, and thus be distinguishable from a real fixational sample. Also, since slower saccades take longer to be completed, they would increase the proportion of samples when the eye was actually moving, rather than fixating, compared with the adult case. Finally, we have discovered that infants sometimes exhibit eye-movement patterns, such as saccadic oscillation or 'back-to-back' saccades, which are rare in normal adults. These oscillations have very brief inter-saccadic intervals, during which the normal processing associated with fixation may not be occurring.

All of these properties of infant eye movements point to the need for a relatively fast sampling rate to isolate reliably those parts of the eye-movement record which are actual fixations. With respect to the studies at issue here, Salapatek (1975) sampled at 4 Hz and regarded each sample as a 'fixation'; Leahy (1976) sampled only once per second (1 Hz). Hainline & Lemerise (1982) sampled eye position 60 times per second; actual fixations were identified by a computer program which defined fixation as relative immobility of the eye, and eye movements as rapid changes of eye position. Sample rates for other studies of infant pattern scanning using corneal reflection techniques are given in Table 1; we have included here only those studies that actually scored eye position quantitatively.

Spatial error.   The other major type of calibration required in eye-movement recording corrects for error in estimating the eye's point of regard in space. The basic principle of such a system requires locating the first Purkinje image, or corneal reflection, of one of a set of light sources of fixed position, relative to some landmark of the eye that changes with eye rotation. In the systems in use with infants, the relevant landmark has been the centre of the pupil. The direction of the eye's optic axis can be derived from this information (e.g. Young & Sheena, 1975). The relationship between the actual and measured eye positions is essentially linear, i.e. 'true' eye position T can be expressed as a linear function of measured eye position M: $T = aM + b$; separate linear functions are needed for the horizontal and vertical coordinates. There are, therefore, two quantities that are important in discussing spatial error in a given direction. The first quantity, gain, refers to how much the eye apparently rotates (as measured by the output of an automated instrument or by a human scorer) when the eye is actually rotated a given amount; the gain term is the multiplicative constant (a) in the linear equation relating obtained and 'true' eye positions. The other quantity corresponds to an offset that is represented by the constant term (b) in the linear equation. To calibrate an individual subject fully, the specific values for the gain and the offset terms need to be established. This is usually accomplished with adults by instructing the subject to look at known locations in space while estimates of eye position are obtained. Equations relating apparent point of regard to true point of regard can then be derived.

Banks & Salapatek (1983) questioned the validity of Hainline & Lemerise's (1982) conclusions on infant scanning for being based upon 'uncalibrated' data. In truth, since the numerical values that a particular instrument or scoring method produces bear no relationship to points in space, any method purporting to specify eye position that was really 'uncalibrated' would be worthless for that purpose. In order to be of any use, the outputs must be related, at least approximately, to positions in space. In the case of work with infants, this initial mapping, effectively establishing an 'average' calibration, is usually based on adult subjects. *Individual* calibrations are then refinements of this 'average' calibration. Hainline & Lemerise's instrument allows an electronic version of this 'average' calibration to be applied to all the data as they are obtained. Hand-scoring methods achieve the same result by creating look-up tables or calibration equations that are applied to the data after they are scored.

It is likely that what Banks & Salapatek meant by their criticism is that we did not have data from each infant to allow an individual calibration equation to be derived for each subject. While this is correct, they neglect to point out that *none* of the studies on infant scanning of simple patterns has corrected the data using individual calibrations.* Thus, problems of interpretation arising from the lack of individual calibration apply equally to all of the studies in Table 1.

---

* Bronson (1982) has presented data that have some individual calibration in the horizontal meridian only. However, since the stimuli he used were more complex than the simple geometric forms that have been used in most of the pattern-scanning studies, and since the 10 infants he tested were 2 months and older, the relevance of his data to these issues is somewhat limited.

Table 1. Quantitative characteristics of corneal reflection systems used to study pattern scanning in infants

Study	Subjects	Sampling rate (Hz)	Uncalibrated spatial accuracy and source of error estimate	Resolution
Salapatek & Kessen (1966)	New-borns	1	Not reported	Approximately 5°
Salapatek (1967, 1969)	New-borns	1	±6°; adult data	Approximately 5° reported (1967)
Salapatek (1969, 1975)	1 & 2 months	3·8	±3–4°; adult data	Not reported
Haith (1969)	New-borns	Videotape; rate not specified	Not reported	Not reported
Kessen et al. (1972)	New-borns	1	Not reported	Not reported
Salapatek et al. (1972)	Adults	1	=4–5°; adult data	Not reported
Salapatek & Kessen (1973)	New-borns	1	Not reported	Not reported
Leahy (1976)	4–6 & 10–12-week infants	1	±6°; adult data	Not reported
Haith et al. (1977)	5–7 & 9–11-week infants / Adults	2 / 3·3	Not reported	Not reported
Haith (1980)	New-borns	2	±4–5°; adult data	Not reported
Hainline (1981b)	1–4-month infants	60	±3–4°; infant and adult data	$\frac{1}{2}$°
Harris (1981)	1–4-month infants	60	=3–4°; infant and adult data	$\frac{1}{2}$°
Hainline & Lemerise (1982)	1–3-month infants	60	±4°; infant data	$\frac{1}{2}$°
Bronson (1982)	2–5-month infants	30	±3–4°; infant data in horizontal meridian only	1–2°

While individual calibration of infants is, in some cases, possible (e.g. Harris *et al.*, 1981; Bronson, 1982), the difficulty of the procedures makes it unlikely that any study will succeed in obtaining such data, in addition to data collected in the actual experiment, from all infant subjects. Given that the lack of individual calibration is the norm in such studies, the critical issue in deciding on the validity of any single study is to evaluate the magnitude of error inherent in eye-position data collected in a given apparatus from subjects who are not individually calibrated. In other words, the sensitivity of a particular recording system or device depends on the appropriateness of the 'average' (usually adult) calibration.

As described above, one of the two relevant terms in the calibration equation is a multiplicative gain term. The relevant parameter in calculating the gain term is usually denoted by k, and is the difference between the radius of curvature of the corneal pole and the distance from the corneal pole to the plane of the entrance pupil (Young & Sheena, 1975; Abramov & Harris, 1984). Bronson (1982, 1983) has reported that the value of k will only increase by about 3 per cent from infancy to adulthood; this conclusion was derived from keratometric (Mandell, 1976) and ultrasonic (Larsen, 1971; Aslin & Jackson, 1979) measures of infant and adult eyes. Although there may be considerable variation in the individual values, the population averages are quite reliable. This analysis means that, in principle, estimates of gain derived from average adults are probably close to those that would be found in infants who are run under identical conditions. A complicating factor is the high degree of corneal astigmatism that has been reported in early infancy (Howland *et al.*, 1978; Mohindra *et al.*, 1978); the effect of this asphericity cannot be corrected by a single gain term, and can produce errors in estimated point of regard that depend on the location of the target in the field.

The major subject-based source of a constant offset is the fact that the optic axis, used as the basis for calculating eye position, and the visual axis, or line of sight, are not exactly the same. In normal adults, the line of sight is determined by the fovea, which is located slightly temporally from the position at which the optic axis intersects the retina. Because of differences in the anatomy of the eyes of infants and adults (Slater & Findlay, 1972, 1975), there may be systematic age-varying offsets in estimating point of regard with corneal reflection techniques, if it is assumed that infants fixate with their central foveas, as adults do. However, recent data (Abramov *et al.*, 1982; Hollyfield *et al.*, 1983) support the claim of older sources (Bach & Seefelder, 1914; Mann, 1964) that foveal portions of the retina may be extremely immature and perhaps not even functional in early infancy. At this point, it is not known whether infants deal with this anatomical immaturity by using some consistent parafoveal area which serves as the 'fovea' for the purpose of directing the eye during fixations; if they do, then this source of offset error would be relatively constant for a given infant. Alternatively, infants could be using a set of 'foveas' in the parafovea, arrayed around the central foveal area. If different areas are used to direct the visual axis at different times, the source of the offset will also be variable. Given the acknowledged variability in the anatomy of the infant eye (Larsen, 1971; Salapatek *et al.*, 1972), and the uncertainty about whether the fovea is functional, it does not seem advisable to apply routinely a fixed correction offset as part of a calibration algorithm.

The eye-movement recording system itself may also have a number of optical sources of error. These include various kinds of parallax error resulting from the relative positions of the head, the camera and the illuminator(s) responsible for the corneal reflection(s). In most cases, these will be constant errors. Since these sources of error are at the same time general and dependent on the exact details of the particular recording device in question, they are not discussed fully here; treatments of the optical sources of error in corneal reflection techniques can be found in several sources (Maurer, 1975; Harris *et al.*, 1981; Sheena & Borah, 1981; Bronson, 1983).

Head movements are a potential source of a variable offset error that is particularly important with infant subjects. Since head movements change the position of the eye with respect to the optics of the eye-tracker, it is possible that head movements may create variable offset errors during a recording session. The magnitude of such errors depends in part on the distances of the infra-red source and the stimulus from the eye, compared with the distance of the eye to the camera (see Bronson, 1983). However, all other factors being equal, the greater the magnification of the eye, the less likely that head-movement artifacts will significantly affect the data; large head movements will move the head from the region where eye position can be scored. Some instruments with automated scoring (e.g. Hainline, 1981*a*) have circuits that compensate for the residual effects of head movements that occur while the eye is still in the field of view of the camera. Another approach to this problem is to record the head movements using tracking mirrors [for example, Bronson (1982) discusses this technique and its associated errors].

Thus the basic sources of error in corneal reflection measurements from infants are similar from apparatus to apparatus, although the magnitude of the various errors will depend on the exact details of each system. At present, only two laboratories (those of Hainline and of Bronson) have collected infant-based calibration data in the scanning paradigm. Bronson (1982) has presented calibration data in the horizontal meridian only, reporting an error of ± 3–$4°$. Our laboratory has published calibration data along with a calibration method for infants (Harris *et al.*, 1981). In the absence of individual calibration data from each infant being run, we have used our calibration data to get estimates of the average spatial error from uncalibrated infants and adults. On average, for both groups, our estimates of absolute spatial position of the eye have an associated spatial error in the order of $\pm 2°$ of visual angle. We have also verified empirically that infant and adult gain factors are similar. Our ability to detect a *change* in eye position between successive samples is of the order of half a degree. The small field of view of our camera requires that the eye be confined to an area less than $2°$ across (or approximately 2 cm in our apparatus) if data are to be obtained. In order to be safe in analysing scanning to patterns, we allow for an error 'margin' of $\pm 4°$ around a figure's contour, since in the *worst* cases (as reported in Hainline, 1981*a*, *b*), error may be as large as this.

Banks & Salapatek (1983) suggest that, with a worst case error of ± 3–$4°$ we were unable to assess the extensiveness of scanning. In Table 1, we present comparative information on the degree of spatial errors in the published studies on pattern scanning using quantitative corneal reflection methods; none has individually calibrated data. In all of those cases in which spatial accuracy is reported, the reported error is at least as large as Hainline & Lemerise's ± 3–$4°$ worst case error and, in many cases, the error is larger. Also, in all of these studies except Hainline & Lemerise (1982) and Bronson (1982), the error estimates are not based on data obtained from infants, but from cooperative adults being instructed to fixate calibration targets. Although the optics of the eye are such that most of the purely optical sources of error should be of an equivalent magnitude for infants and adults as discussed above, there are other factors (such as the degree of corneal astigmatism and other anatomical differences in infant and adult eyes) which make infant-based calibration data an important source of information to validate error estimates obtained from adults. Reference to Table 1 also shows that, since most systems have a very low sampling rate, it is difficult to estimate the relative resolution for detecting a change in eye position between two successive samples. Faster systems which have reasonably high resolution provide information about the spatial relationships between successive samples that is lost with low sample rates.

From Table 1 it can be seen that *all* of the studies of infant pattern scanning use data that have not been individually calibrated. Thus, citing the lack of calibration as a basis for excluding studies relevant to whether there are developmental differences in pattern scanning seems not to be a sensible tactic. A more critical question is whether all of the methods are so inaccurate in estimating an infant's eye position as to be of little value in studies of infant scanning. As we have indicated, *no* systems in use with infants are error-free and the problem of calibrating such systems for use with infants is one with which all researchers using the technique continue to struggle. However, we have not reviewed many of the problems and sources of error associated with the technique in order to imply that the method has no utility. The essential point is that a system's error of measurement needs to 'fit' the research question being asked. One needs a very different level of resolution if studying microsaccades than if one is asking about scanning to forms that are many degrees across. For example, Banks & Salapatek's criticism of our system's accuracy is used to imply that our system's resolution is not good enough to detect developmental differences in scanning extensiveness; however, our system was 'precise' enough to pick up a very consistent change in scanning as a function of stimulus size, for stimuli 5–30° across. Were there an age trend in scanning extensiveness, it would have been precise enough to reveal it as well.

Absolute vs. relative scanning extensiveness

In their review of the infant pattern-scanning literature, Banks & Salapatek distinguished between two types of scanning extensiveness: 'absolute extensiveness', in which scanning extensiveness is unrelated to parts of the figure, and 'relative extensiveness', in which scanning extensiveness is assessed relative to parts of a figure. They suggest that the reason why no developmental trends were found in Hainline & Lemerise (1982) was because we failed to measure 'relative extensiveness'. However, such a distinction between the two kinds of extensiveness was not articulated prior to the 1983 review. None of the earlier studies, including Leahy (1976) or Salapatek (1975), provides an objective, quantitative test of developmental changes in relative extensiveness. Indeed, most of the analyses in the published work on neonates (e.g. Salapatek & Kessen, 1966, 1973; Salapatek, 1968) are of absolute, rather than relative extensiveness. Nevertheless, with respect to their criticism of the Hainline & Lemerise (1982) study, using the 1983 definitions, it is strictly true that that study had no direct measure of 'relative extensiveness'.* There were a number of indirect measures that would have revealed an age trend if one were present.

However, in order to satisfy the new definition of 'relative extensiveness', we have undertaken a reanalysis of all of the data presented in our 1982 paper. Previously we had evaluated the overall variance of the *x* and *y* coordinates of fixation position (unrelated to the stimulus) and also the proportion of fixations that fell in different regions of the stimulus. In that analysis, three regions were defined: 'on-contour' (fixations falling within a ±4° boundary of the figure's contour), 'centre of stimulus' (the region inside the contour region), and 'off-stimulus' (the region outside the contour region). 'On-stimulus' fixations fell either in the stimulus centre or in the contour region. It should be noted that all of these analyses used the coordinates of actual fixations, not time-sampled measures of ocular orientation, as in Salapatek (1975). In all of these analyses, figure size had a significant effect, whereas subject age (1, 2 and 3 months) did not. In our reanalysis, we examined those fixations which fell in specific stimulus regions, i.e. centre, contour, off-stimulus and on-stimulus (centre plus contour). The dispersion (variance) of the *x* and *y*

---

* One of our analyses evaluated the proportion of fixations in each quadrant of the stimulus screen (irrespective of the particular stimulus being presented); this analysis was designed to check if infants had detected the illuminator providing the corneal reflection. Banks & Salapatek considered this analysis as a possible measure of relative extensiveness and argue that it is incorrect as such. In this they are correct, but these analyses were done to control for a possible artifact, not as a measure of scanning extensiveness.

coordinates of fixation position was calculated separately for each of these regions for each subject. Since these variances could not be assumed to be normally distributed, they were rank ordered across subjects and stimulus size, and non-parametric analyses of variance of ranks were performed. The ranks of the variances are presented in Table 2. If 2-month-olds show greater relative extensiveness than 1-month-olds, as the earlier studies claimed, they should have had higher average ranks than the younger infants for the variance of their contour or on-stimulus fixations (i.e. only those which are 'figure-related'). As the results in Table 2 show, there was no significant difference among age groups in 'relative extensiveness' by this measure. As before, the robust effects of stimulus size on infant scanning are obvious, while age is not a significant factor in these measures. Regressions of these variables on infant age in days (as opposed to grouping infants into three age categories as in the analyses of variance of ranks) also failed to yield significant age effects.

Conclusions

Where does this leave us? Our review of the calibration issue and the reanalysis of our 1982 data both serve to weaken Banks & Salapatek's conclusions about the pattern-scanning literature. Rather than there being clear evidence for a developmental trend in pattern scanning, the results of Hainline & Lemerise (1982) in combination with work on new-born habituation (e.g. Slater *et al.*, 1982), suggest that such a trend is not well supported. What then of the discrepancies between the earlier studies and our own? In 1982, we suggested several possible reasons why our data might be at variance with those published previously, particularly with the studies on infants beyond the neonatal period (Salapatek, 1969, 1975; Leahy, 1976).

(1) In the earlier work, scanning of younger infants might have been 'narrow' because the stimuli used may have been so large that oculo-motor and attentional constraints prevented the infants from appreciating the 'wholeness' of the shape, or the stimuli may have been so large that they went beyond the effective visual fields of the younger infants.

(2) In the Salapatek study, the infra-red illuminators used to photograph the eye and produce the corneal reflections may have been visible and could have been the target to which the younger infants were attending; we pointed out the tendency in the Salapatek study for many infants to show a heavy concentration of scanning in the same general location, regardless of which figure was the stimulus. This unusual behaviour is consistent with an environmental artifact. Indeed, in earlier neonatal studies (Salapatek & Kessen, 1966; Salapatek, 1968; Nelson & Kessen, 1969) it was noted that when infra-red illuminators of the eye-tracker were located at the vertices of a large triangle, neonates tended to scan vertices, while when the illuminators were located on the sides of the stimulus, sides were scanned more extensively. If 2-month-olds scanned more extensively in the Salapatek (1969, 1975) study, it may have been because of changes for the older infants in the salience of the faintly visible red illuminators relative to other features of the stimulus.

(3) Finally, the infants in the Salapatek (1969, 1975) and in the Leahy (1976) studies were lying down on their backs and were given pacifiers to steady their heads. Hainline & Lemerise noted that the limitation of scanning to a very small spatial locus was consistent with the behaviour of the infant in a state of non-alert waking, a 'trance-like' state in which the eyes are open but the infant does not appear to be processing incoming information (e.g. Wolff, 1966; Korner, 1972; Prechtl, 1982). Data from other studies have shown that pacifiers can reduce visual exploration and responsiveness (Bruner, 1973; Macfarlane *et al.*, 1976). The infants in the Hainline & Lemerise (1982) study were upright, a position in which infants are more likely to be alert than in the supine position (Korner & Thoman, 1970; Bower, 1971); also, infants were not given pacifiers. Thus we argued that in our study

Table 2. Main effects of non-parametric analyses of variance of ranks for fixation position in stimulus regions

Region	Size			Effect (P<)	Age (months)			Effect
	Small	Medium	Large		1	2	3	
Variance of horizontal position in contour region	32·694	55·986	74·819	0·0001	55·542	55·167	52·792	n.s.
Variance of vertical position in contour region	30·833	58·431	74·236	0·0001	57·875	55·972	49·653	n.s.
Proportion of fixations in contour region	33·083	57·639	72·778	0·0001	58·611	57·181	47·708	n.s.
Variance of horizontal position in centre region[a]	—	32·361	40·639	0·0481	35·708	38·125	35·667	n.s.
Variance of vertical position in centre region[a]	—	33·111	39·889	n.s.	34·167	39·083	36·250	n.s.
Proportion of fixations in centre region[a]	—	29·500	43·500	0·0009	34·271	36·896	38·333	n.s.
Variance of horizontal position on-stimulus	30·889	55·014	77·597	0·0001	56·403	54·556	52·542	n.s.
Variance of vertical position on-stimulus	29·667	56·056	77·778	0·0001	56·069	55·764	51·667	n.s.
Proportion of fixations on-stimulus	29·944	56·764	76·792	0·0001	56·528	57·889	49·083	n.s.

Note. All values reported are ranks.
[a] In the small (5°) form there was no centre region after the contour region was subtracted.

the younger infants, whose states of alertness are briefer and more labile than those of older infants, may have been visually more alert than subjects in the earlier studies.

There are technical reasons which may have caused a difference in the proportion of alert subjects run in the earlier studies and in Hainline & Lemerise (1982). Early methods of scoring eye position, as in Salapatek (1975), consisted of having a human observer detect the pupil centre and the corneal reflection. The lighting conditions in those studies resulted in an image of the eye with a dark pupil. In the more recent automated scoring systems, in order to facilitate detection of the pupil by the image-detecting circuitry, the eye is illuminated with a collimated light source co-axial with the eye and the camera to create a 'bright' pupil image. In the automatic detection systems, if the pupil is too constricted or the amount of light being reflected back from the retina is too small, as can happen in a subject with relaxed accommodation, the pupil cannot be detected reliably and no estimates of eye position can be obtained. Pupil constriction and relaxed accommodation are two characteristics that accompany a reduced state of arousal in infants (Fitzgerald, 1968; Banks, 1980). With the human scorer and the dark pupil method, estimates of eye position would in most cases continue to be derived from drowsy infants, leading to proportionally more data from non-alert infants. Hainline & Lemerise (1982) had to test 111 infants to get reasonably complete data from 36 subjects; our experiment took 90 seconds to complete (without breaks), and it was observed that many infants found the stimuli less than fascinating. Salapatek (1969, 1975) does not specify how many subjects were tested to achieve the published data-base, but the total minimum stimulus presentation time, including inter-stimulus intervals, was at least 10 minutes. (This does not include any breaks in data collection.) Given the above considerations, we feel that Salapatek may have been testing drowsy babies, particularly at 1 month.

Finally, it should also be noted that the earlier claims were based on a qualitative judgement of how the infants in the two age groups scanned; no standard statistical analyses have been presented to establish the validity of the claim of a developmental effect.

Criteria for evaluating corneal reflection studies

We have been quite critical of the corneal reflection method in this paper, but we do not mean to imply that the technique has no value in infant research. Salapatek and his colleagues, particularly Kessen and Haith, have provided us with a valuable and potentially powerful tool for studying the visual functioning of young infants. Despite the difficulties inherent in the method, we believe its real potential remains to be tapped. We do feel, however, that some of the early work with the method, seen from the distance of more than a decade, may have been overly enthusiastic about the ability of the method to assess directly the level of infants' visual functions. Without considering other aspects of infant behaviour—such as behavioural state and the individual infant's cognitive 'preparation' for whichever stimulus was being shown—the meaning of the data on infant scanning is ambiguous at best. Further, some of the work relied too heavily on qualitative analyses in drawing conclusions, a particular irony given that the work is among the most technically demanding and sophisticated to have been attempted with infants.

We suggest that research on visual processing in infants using corneal reflection techniques should be evaluated in terms of the following questions in order to ascertain whether the data reflect the characteristics of visual processing:

(1) Is there evidence that the infant is alert enough for scanning to be taken as a reflection of cognitive processing?

(2) Has the error of measurement been estimated and is its magnitude appropriate to the research question being addressed?

(3) Could some unintended aspect of the environment be the stimulus to which the infant is actually responding? In order to relate the infants' scanning to the characteristics of the stimulus, one must be able to rule out environmental artifacts, such as the infra-red illuminator(s) or other parts of the apparatus, as determinants of the infants' fixations; this is most easily done by evaluating whether there is an unusually high concentration of fixations to the spatial locations that these items occupy.

(4) Can scanning be shown to be related to the stimulus? There is a natural tendency for the eyes to be positioned centrally near a location called the 'primary position', in the absence of stimuli that draw the eye away from the straight ahead position. Thus, evidence that the infant fixates the central visual field during a trial when a stimulus is presented straight ahead is not unequivocal evidence that scanning is stimulus-related. To be certain that the nature of the stimulus is important for scanning, one should be able to demonstrate that changing some aspect of the stimulus results in a change in some aspect of scanning.

(5) Have the data been quantitatively analysed in appropriate ways? Does the precision of analysis match the precision of recording? Qualitative analyses must be regarded as of questionable validity until their validity has been established by standard quantitative statistical methods.

Unfortunately much of the early work fails to meet one or more of these criteria, so that we argue here that less is known about infant scanning and what this behaviour implies about infant development than has conventionally been concluded in standard reviews of the topic. Our reanalysis of our own data and of the results and methods of the small number of extant studies on infant pattern scanning fails to support the conclusion that clear developmental trends in pattern scanning can be demonstrated in a child's first three months. Further studies in this demanding research area should pay careful attention to the concerns described here in order to maximize the utility of information collected on these infant abilities.

Acknowledgements

We thank Israel Abramov, Christopher Harris and Alan Slater for their helpful discussions. This research was supported by National Institute of Health grants HD08706 and EY03957, and by awards Nos 661078, 662199 and 663127 from the PSC–CUNY Research Award Program of the City University of New York. Facilities for data analysis were provided by the CUNY University Computer Center. We thank Drs Max Lilling and David Kliot and Downstate Medical Center for assisting us in locating subjects. We also thank the infants and their parents for giving us their time.
    Much of the content of this article can be construed as a critique of early work by the late Phil Salapatek. We believe that Dr Salapatek would have appreciated the spirit in which this analysis is offered and would have seen it as an attempt to improve a research method that he pioneered.

References

Abramov, I., Gordon, J., Hendrickson, A., Hainline, L., Dobson, V. & LaBossiere, E. (1982). The retina of the newborn human infant. *Science*, **217**, 265–267.
Abramov, I. & Harris, C. M. (1984). Artificial eye for assessing corneal-reflection eye trackers. *Behavior Research Methods, Instruments, and Computers*, **16**, 341–350.
Aslin, R. N. (1981). Development of smooth pursuit in human infants. In D. F. Fisher, R. A. Monty & J. W. Senders (eds), *Eye Movements: Cognition and Visual Perception*, pp. 31–52. Hillsdale, NJ: Erlbaum.
Aslin, R. N. & Jackson, R. W. (1979). Accommodative-convergence in young infants: Development of a synergistic sensory-motor system. *Canadian Journal of Psychology*, **33**, 222–231.
Bach, L. & Seefelder, R. (1914). *Atlas zur Entwicklungsgeschichte des menschlichen Auges*. Leipzig: Engelmann.
Banks, M. (1980). The development of visual accommodation during early infancy. *Child Development*, **51**, 646–666.
Banks, M. & Salapatek, P. (1983). Infant visual perception. In M. Haith & J. Campos (eds), *Biology and Infancy*. P. Mussen (ed.), *Handbook of Child Psychology*. New York: Wiley.
Bower, T. G. R. (1971). The object in the world of the infant. *Scientific American*, **225**, 30–38.

Bronson, G. (1974). The postnatal growth of visual capacity. *Child Development*, **45**, 873–890.
Bronson, G. (1982). *The Scanning Patterns of Human Infants: Implications for Visual Learning*. Norwood, NJ: Ablex.
Bronson, G. W. (1983). Potential sources of error when applying a corneal reflex eye-monitoring technique to infant subjects. *Behavior Research Methods and Instrumentation*, **15**, 22–28.
Bruner, J. S. (1973). Pacifier-produced visual buffering in human infants. *Developmental Psychobiology*, **6**, 45–51.
Cohen, L. B. & Gelber, E. R. (1975). Infant visual memory. In L. B. Cohen & P. Salapatek (eds), *Infant Perception: From Sensation to Cognition*, vol. 1, pp. 347–403. New York: Academic Press.
Fitzgerald, H. E. (1968). Autonomic pupillary reflex activity during early infancy and its relation to social and nonsocial visual stimuli. *Journal of Experimental Child Psychology*, **6**, 470–482.
Hainline, L. (1981a). An automated eye movement recording system for use with human infants. *Behavior Research Methods and Instrumentation*, **13**, 20–24.
Hainline, L. (1981b). Eye movements and form perception in human infants. In D. F. Fisher, R. A. Monty & J. W. Senders (eds), *Eye Movements: Cognition and Visual Perception*, pp. 3–19. Hillsdale, NJ: Erlbaum.
Hainline, L. (1984). Saccades in human infants. In A. G. Gale & C. W. Johnson (eds), *Theoretical and Applied Aspects of Eye Movement Research*, pp. 273–280. Amsterdam: North-Holland.
Hainline, L. & Lemerise, E. (1982). Infants' scanning of geometric forms varying in size. *Journal of Experimental Child Psychology*, **33**, 235–256.
Hainline, L., Turkel, J., Abramov, I., Lemerise, E. & Harris, C. M. (1984). Characteristics of saccades in human infants. *Vision Research*, **24**, 1771–1780.
Haith, M. M. (1969). Infrared television recording and measurement of ocular behavior in the human infant. *American Psychologist*, **24**, 279–282.
Haith, M. M. (1980). *Rules that Babies Look by: The Organization of Newborn Visual Activity*. Hillsdale, NJ: Erlbaum.
Haith, M. M., Bergman, T. & Moore, M. J. (1977). Eye contact and face scanning in early infancy. *Science*, **198**, 853–856.
Harris, C. M., Abramov, I. & Hainline, L. (1984). Instrument considerations in measuring fast eye movements. *Behavior Research Methods, Instruments, and Computers*, **16**, 341–350.
Harris, C. M., Hainline, L. & Abramov, I. (1981). A method for calibrating an eye-monitoring system for use with human infants. *Behavior Research Methods and Instrumentation*, **13**, 11–20.
Hollyfield, J. G., Frederick, J. M. & Rayborn, M. E. (1983). Neurotransmitter properties in the newborn human retina. *Investigative Ophthalmology and Visual Science*, **24**, 893–897.
Howland, H. C., Atkinson, J., Braddick, O. & French, J. (1978). Infant astigmatism measured by photorefraction. *Science*, **202**, 331–332.
Kessen, W., Salapatek, P. & Haith, M. M. (1972). The visual response of the human infant to linear contour. *Journal of Experimental Child Psychology*, **13**, 9–20.
Korner, A. F. (1972). State as variable, as obstacle, and as mediator of stimulation in infant research. *Merrill-Palmer Quarterly*, **18**, 77–94.
Korner, A. F. & Thoman, E. (1970). Visual alertness in neonates as evoked by maternal care. *Journal of Experimental Child Psychology*, **10**, 67–78.
Larsen, J. S. (1971). The sagittal growth of the eye. I. Ultrasonic measurement of the depth of the anterior chamber from birth to puberty. *Acta Ophthalmologica*, **49**, 239–262.
Leahy, R. L. (1976). Development of preferences and processes of visual scanning in the human infant during the first 3 months of life. *Developmental Psychology*, **12**, 250–254.
MacFarlane, A., Harris, P. & Barnes, I. (1976). Central and peripheral vision in early infancy. *Journal of Experimental Child Psychology*, **21**, 532–538.
Mandell, R. B. (1976). Corneal curvature of the human infant. *Archives of Ophthalmology*, **77**, 345–348.
Mann, I. (1964). *The Development of the Human Eye*. London: British Medical Association.
Maurer, D. (1975). Infant visual perception: Methods of study. In L. B. Cohen & P. Salapatek (eds), *Infant Perception: From Sensation to Cognition*, vol. 1, pp. 1–76. New York: Academic Press.
Mohindra, I., Held, R., Gwiazda, J. & Brill, S. (1978). Astigmatism in infants. *Science*, **202**, 329–330.
Nelson, K. & Kessen, W. (1969). Visual scanning by human newborns: Responses to complete triangle, to sides only, and to corners only. *Proceedings of the 77th Annual Convention of the American Psychological Association*.
Prechtl, H. F. (1982). Assessment methods for the newborn infant, a critical evaluation. In P. Stratton (ed.), *Psychobiology of the Human Newborn*, pp. 21–52. New York: Wiley.
Salapatek, P. (1967). Visual scanning of geometric figures by the human newborn. PhD dissertation, Yale University. Ann Arbor, MI: University Microfilms International.
Salapatek, P. (1968). Visual scanning of geometric figures by the human newborn. *Journal of Comparative and Physiological Psychology*, **66**, 247–258.
Salapatek, P. (1969). The visual investigation of geometric patterns by the one- and two-month-old infant. Paper presented at Meeting of the American Association for the Advancement of Science, Boston, MA.
Salapatek, P. (1975). Pattern perception in early infancy. In L. B. Cohen & P. Salapatek (eds), *Infant Perception: From Sensation to Cognition*, vol. 1, pp. 133–248. New York: Academic Press.
Salapatek, P., Haith, M. M., Maurer, D. A. & Kessen, W. (1972). Error in the corneal reflection technique: A note on Slater and Findlay. *Journal of Experimental Child Psychology*, **14**, 493–497.

Salapatek, P. & Kessen, W. (1966). Visual scanning of triangles by the human newborn. *Journal of Experimental Child Psychology*, **3**, 155–167.

Salapatek, P. & Kessen, W. (1973). Prolonged investigation of a plane geometric triangle by the human newborn. *Journal of Experimental Child Psychology*, **15**, 22–29.

Sheena, D. & Borah, J. (1981). Compensation for some second order effects to improve eye position measurements. In D. F. Fisher, R. A. Monty & J. W. Senders (eds), *Eye Movements: Cognition and Visual Perception*, pp. 257–270. Hillsdale, NJ: Erlbaum.

Slater, A. M. & Findlay, J. M. (1972). The measurement of fixation position in the newborn baby. *Journal of Experimental Child Psychology*, **14**, 349–366.

Slater, A. M. & Findlay, J. M. (1975). The corneal reflection technique and the visual preference method: Sources of error. *Journal of Experimental Child Psychology*, **20**, 240–247.

Slater, A., Morison, V. & Rose, D. (1982). Visual memory at birth. *British Journal of Psychology*, **73**, 519–525.

Slater, A., Morison, V. & Rose, D. (1983a). Locus of habituation in the human newborn. *Perception*, **12**, 593–598.

Slater, A., Morison, V. & Rose, D. (1983b). Perception of shape by the human newborn baby. *British Journal of Developmental Psychology*, **1**, 135–142.

Slater, A., Morison, V. & Rose, D. (1984). Habituation in the newborn. *Infant Behavior and Development*, **7**, 183–200.

Slater, A., Morison, V. & Rose, D. (1985). Movement perception and identity constancy in the newborn baby. *British Journal of Developmental Psychology*, **3**, 211–220.

Wolff, P. H. (1966). The causes, controls and organization of behavior in the neonate. *Psychological Issues*, **5**, Whole no. 17.

Young, L. R. & Sheena, D. (1975). Eye-movement measurement techniques. *American Psychologist*, **30**, 315–330.

Requests for reprints should be addressed to Dr Louise Hainline, Department of Psychology, Brooklyn College of the City University of New York, Brooklyn, New York 11210, USA.

Elizabeth Lemerise is also at the above address.

British Journal of Developmental Psychology (1985), **3**, 243–258   *Printed in Great Britain*   243 [35]

A longitudinal study of the development of the object concept

Jennifer G. Wishart and T. G. R. Bower

Object concept development was studied longitudinally in a group of 24 infants from 12 weeks until achievement of Stage 6. Infants were tested between 12 and 28 weeks on four visual tracking tasks: a simple, unoccluded tracking task and three others, each involving a different spatial relationship in mid-track between the object and an occluder (a screen, tunnel, or platform). Competence on manual search tasks was monitored from the age at which reaching first appeared. Understanding of the same three spatial relationships between object and occluder (behind, in and on) was tested. Early exposure to the visual tracking tasks turned out to have a substantial accelerative effect on object concept development. Both the visual and manual data collected lend more support to a three-advance identity model of object concept development than to the traditional six-stage Piagetian model.

This paper presents a longitudinal study of the development of the object concept from Stages 1–6. So far as we know, it is the first such study since Piaget's classic presentation of the behaviour of his own three children (Piaget, 1936, 1937). There are, allegedly, six stages in the development of the object concept. There have been very many studies, both cross-sectional and longitudinal, of the Stage 4–5 transition error (e.g. Butterworth, 1977; Bremner, 1978), a few studies of the Stages 4, 5 and 6 sequence (e.g. Miller *et al.*, 1970; Gratch & Landers, 1971; Wishart & Bower, 1984) and even fewer studies of the earliest stages, Stages 1, 2 and 3 (e.g. Bower *et al.*, 1971; Mundy-Castle & Anglin, 1973). Indeed, there is as yet no general acceptance that all six stages reflect a common developmental sequence (Harris, 1984), although Bower & Paterson (1972) have presented what they feel is strong evidence in favour of a unitary developmental process.

A problem in the study of the whole sequence of development of the object concept is that the indicator behaviours that can be used change with age. In essence, the changes in the early Stages can only be marked by changes in visual tracking. The later changes, by contrast, can be, and usually are, measured by examination of visually directed, manual search. Study of the developmental sequence in two halves has led to theoretical problems. For example, at one level of description manual search appears to repeat errors overcome months earlier in purely visual search. Thus a baby younger than 20 weeks will search with its eyes for an object where it has seen it before, disregarding its visible movement to a completely different location; similarly, up to 10 or 11 months, a baby will search with its hands for an object where it has found it before, disregarding its visible transport to a completely different place (Bower, 1974*a*). This can be seen as evidence that the sequence is no sequence or as evidence for a process of *décalage* (Piaget, 1967) between eye movement and hand movement, with task demand and information load the obstructing variables (Bower, 1967; Willatts, 1979) It was thought that a longitudinal study might answer some of these problems.

The general theory of development of the object concept that directed design and analysis was the identity theory proposed by Bower (Bower, 1974*b*; Wishart & Bower, 1984). Many theories have focused on representation of invisible objects, with 'out of sight, out of mind' the main explanatory axiom. Piaget (1936, 1937) himself showed that a general theory of this kind would not do. Subsequently it has been shown that invisibility is neither a necessary (Bower, 1967; Bresson & de Schonen, 1977; Butterworth, 1977; Neilson, 1982) nor a sufficient (Bower & Wishart, 1973) condition for the elicitation of the behaviours that mark the emergence of the object concept. Identity theory by contrast focuses on the rules the baby uses to identify an object as one and the same object across time and space. The youngest infants are presumed to identify an object either as a bounded volume of space in a particular location or as a bounded volume of space on a particular path of movement (identity rule 1). The first advance comes when the baby identifies an object as a bounded volume of space that can move from place to place (identity rule 2). At this Stage the baby still cannot cope with spatial relations that involve boundary loss, so that when an object is placed on/in/behind/in front of/ etc. another object, both lose their identity and are, in the baby's mind, replaced by a single new object, object-plus-occluder. The second advance comes with the realization that one object can go into spatial relation with another with both retaining their separate existence (identity rule 3). The third and last advance comes when the child realizes that, under some circumstances, two objects in particular spatial relation will share one another's movements or displacements. In the studies reported here this last transition was not studied by visual tracking. Likewise no attempt was made to study manual behaviour prior to the first advance.

Method

Subjects

Twenty-four subjects, 11 male, 13 female, were divided into two groups, E1 and E2. All were 12 weeks of age on beginning the experiment.

Design and procedure

Both groups, E1 and E2, visited the laboratory at weekly intervals from 12 to 28 weeks. Any sessions which had to be prematurely terminated were resumed in the same week where possible. Two sessions took place in the 28th week of testing. Tracking tasks were begun at 12 weeks and given at weekly intervals thereafter. Reaching tasks were started on the week in which the baby first demonstrated the ability to reach and touch a dangling object within 2 minutes of its presentation. From then on, both tracking and reaching tasks were given in each session. The tracking tasks always preceded the reaching tasks. Half of the subjects, E1, went on at 29 weeks to participate in a longitudinal egocentrism study (Wishart & Bower, 1982). The other half, E2, transferred to a related tracking/reaching study undertaken by Neilson (1977). Both groups continued to be monitored on the Stage 4–6 manual tasks, monthly and fortnightly respectively.

A. *Tracking tasks*
In the tracking tasks, infants sat on their mothers' laps, facing the display and at a distance of 3 feet from it. Where necessary, the mother would support the infant's head under the chin. Mothers were instructed not to direct the baby's attention in any way but to allow him or her to look at whichever part of the display he or she chose. Sessions were video-recorded for subsequent frame-by-frame analysis. A T5 camera mounted behind the display and out of sight of the infant monitored head and eye movements while object position was simultaneously monitored by a camera above the display.
   Four tracking presentations were used (see Fig. 1):
1. *Simple tracking*: The object travelled from X to Y, paused for 3 seconds (trial 1), travelled back to X, paused at X for a further 3 seconds (trial 2), and so on.
2. *Platform tracking* (on): As in 1, but passing over a platform positioned midway between X and Y. The platform was constructed out of the same material as the tracking apparatus (chipboard) and was 8 in long. It was of such a height that the base of the object just touched it as it passed over it. The object therefore effectively lost its bottom boundary on crossing the platform.
3. *Screen tracking* (behind): As in 1, but passing behind a screen positioned midway between X and Y. The screen was constructed of the same material as the tracking apparatus, measured 8 × 8 in and stood $\frac{1}{2}$ in front of the track.
4. *Tunnel tracking* (in): As in 1, but passing through a tunnel positioned midway between X and Y. The tunnel was made of lightweight, opaque, grey plastic, was 8 in long and 3 in in diameter.
   The same object, a red, fluorescent polystyrene block, $2 \times 1\frac{1}{2} \times 1$ in, was used in all presentations. The object was carried on a fine link chain, driven by a Bodine motor. Speed of movement of the object was 3·2 in/s. The length of the track was 36 in. Each trial therefore lasted 11·25 s, with a 3 s pause at either end of the track. In conditions

2–4, the length of the occluder* was 8 in; duration of occlusion was therefore 2·5 s. The process of occlusion itself took 0·6 s.

Presentation began when the infant first noticed the moving object or after four full excursions, whichever was the sooner. Presentation of any one condition consisted of eight complete trials thereafter. On alternate weeks, two stop trials were incorporated, one after the fourth trial, one after the eighth trial. In the first stop trial, the object stopped in approximately the middle of the first section (A) of unoccluded track (i.e. *before* entering the tunnel, going on to the platform, etc.); on the second stop trial, it stopped in approximately the middle of the second section (B) of unoccluded track (i.e. *after* emerging from the tunnel, coming off the platform, etc.). The stop position was not more exactly controlled since it was felt necessary to introduce a degree of flexibility in order to cover those instances where the infant did not track section A or B in its entirety. Stop duration was 5 s.

Each baby saw two of the four tracking conditions weekly. All possible pairs of conditions were used, in both orders of presentation. Conditions were paired and sequenced such that a total of 12 babies saw each of the four conditions at each week level and each individual baby on average saw all four conditions every fortnight, the

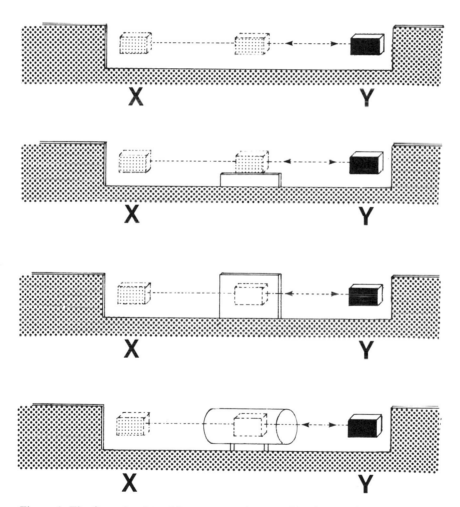

Figure 1. The four visual tracking presentations used in the experiment—from top to bottom: the simple unoccluded tracking task, the platform tracking task (on), the screen tracking task (behind), the tunnel tracking task (inside).

---

* The form 'occluder' and 'occluded' is used throughout in reference to condition 2, as well as conditions 3 and 4. In condition 2, the platform condition, the object is not 'occluded' in the true sense of the word; it would appear however that when an object goes over a platform, temporarily losing its bottom boundary, something equivalent happens as far as the infant is concerned (see Results section).

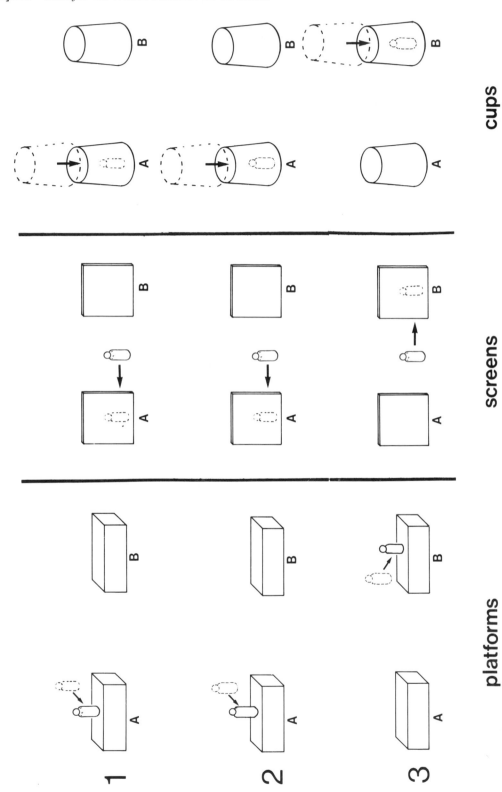

Figure 2. The three Stage 3–5 reaching tasks used in the experiment—from left to right: the platform reaching task, the screen reaching task, the cup reaching task.

maximum separation between two presentations of the same condition being three weeks. For group E1, stop trials took place on even-age weeks; for E2, on odd-age weeks. There was therefore stop data for six babies on each of the four conditions at each week level. At 28 weeks, each baby saw his/her appropriate pair of conditions and then returned later that week to see the remaining two conditions.

B. *Reaching tasks*

Reaching tasks were started in the week the baby first demonstrated the ability to reach and touch a dangling object within a time limit of 2 min. In the reaching tasks, infants sat on their mothers' laps at a table which had a semicircular cut-out on the infant's side to facilitate reaching. Mothers were asked to support the infants in such a way as to neither restrict nor direct their reaching and to restrain their infants from reaching while the object was in the process of being hidden.

Three reaching tasks were used (see Fig. 2):

1. *Platform reaching* (on): The object was placed slowly on one of two platforms made of white, high-density, plastic foam, 4 in square and 2 in high, positioned 6 in apart and at an equal distance from the baby. If the baby was successful in removing the object from the platform within 2 min, the same object was again placed on that platform (A). If again successful, the object was then placed on the other platform (B) [i.e. a Stage 4–5 (AAB)] sequence, with the first trial constituting a Stage 3–4 test in the event of a Stage 5 failure). On B trials, a short delay (1 s) was introduced between hiding and search (see Gratch *et al.*, 1974). Care was taken that the infant attended to each part of the sequence.
2. *Screen reaching* (behind): AAB sequence as in 1 but object hidden behind one of two screens made of white, non-reflective card and measuring 5 × 5 in (a size which made it impossible for the infant to see the object over the top of the screen but was still relatively easy to remove).
3. *Cup reaching* (inside): AAB sequence as in 1 but object hidden inside one of two cups made of blue cardboard, 4 in high and 3 in diameter (suitable white cups were unavailable).

These three reaching tasks obviously involve the same three spatial relationships between object and occluder as in the tracking presentations.

The aim was to give each baby two AAB sequences, one starting on the baby's left, one on the right, of each of the three reaching tasks. In the early weeks of reaching, however, reaching or attempting to reach is a laborious and difficult process for infants and they rapidly become very tired. Consequently, order of presentation of the tasks was chosen to maximize the possibility of at least some response (though not necessarily successful recovery of the object) occurring to more than one condition. Order was therefore reduced to a function of two rather than three variables, platform and cup or screen, the assumption being that, in the case of the platform, as the object was still in sight, attention would at least be retained to some extent although reaching might not necessarily follow. It was hoped that such a procedure would increase the chance of being able to test more than one condition in these early weeks. Half of the infants therefore did the task in the order platform, followed by cup or screen, half doing the reverse order. Within the cup or screen variable, half would start with cup, half with screen. There were therefore six babies in each of the four groups, PS, SP, CP and PC, chosen equally from the two original tracking groups E1 and E2 (where P = platform, S = screen and C = cup).

Two AAB sequences of the first task would be given, one starting on the left, one on the right (randomly assigned). Then, one AAB sequence of the next task would be given. If the baby was still interested and responsive, one AAB sequence of the remaining task (always a cup or screen task) would be given starting on the side opposite to the previous task. If, after all this, the baby was still attentive and happy, the remaining tasks would be given. The following week, the infant would start with the other of the two possibilities and proceed as above. (If the first condition was screen or cup, the infant would do whichever one had been third in the previous week. Week 3 was as week 1 and so on.) As it turned out, infants were soon able to get through all three conditions in the one session so the above precautions became superfluous. Adoption of this procedure did, however, mean that a reasonable spread of data was obtained during the early weeks of reaching.

On all trials, infants were given time (and encouragement) to correct any mistakes they made. If they failed to do so the experimenter drew their attention to the correct location, removed the occluder and gave the infant the object. Where possible, the same object, a brightly coloured wooden doll, was used throughout the reaching presentations. When it became obvious that this no longer interested the baby, another object would be substituted. All objects were brightly coloured, flat-based and approximately 1½–2 in in height and 1 in in width. If an infant lost interest in the object while within any AAB sequence, that sequence would be abandoned and a new sequence and new object introduced.

At 28 weeks, group E1 moved into a longitudinal egocentrism study while group E2 moved on into a further longitudinal tracking/reaching study (see above). Both groups continued to be monitored at fortnightly or monthly intervals on the Stage 4–6 manual object concept tasks. Stages 4 and 5 were assessed as above while Stage 6 was tested by the Stage 5–6 transition task (Fig. 3—see also Wishart & Bower, 1984). In this task, the object was placed under one of two identical cups and the position of the two cups then transposed, a procedure which resulted in the invisible displacement of the object from left to right or vice versa. Six trials were given, three with the object's initial hiding position on the infant's left, three on the right. Within this restriction, order of initial hiding position was randomly assigned for each infant.

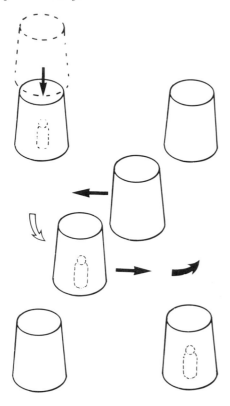

Figure 3. The Stage 5–6 transition task.

Results

Analysis: Tracking tasks

Condition 1, simple tracking, was analysed for two features only: complete or partial tracking and smooth or confused tracking. Confusion was defined as tracking back or forward to some point on the track other than that at which the object was clearly visible. Looking off to any area of the visual field other than the track was scored as inattention.

For conditions 2–4 (platform/screen/tunnel tracking) tracking trials were divided into five time periods for analysis as follows:
1. object on first section of unoccluded track (A);
2. disappearance of object, i.e. from when object first goes on to platform/behind screen/into tunnel until it is completely occluded;
3. object completely occluded;
4. reappearance of object, i.e. when object first reappears from platform/screen/tunnel until completely reappeared;
5. object on second section of unoccluded track (B).

Using frame-by-frame analysis, records were scored for the following nine responses:
1. looks off;
2. tracks forward (terminus of track noted);
3. tracks forward to exit;
4. tracks forward past exit (terminus of track noted);
5. tracks back (terminus of track noted);
6. tracks back to entry;

7. tracks back to exit;
8. stops at exit;
9. stops at entry.

Although several of these responses are appropriate responses to demonstrate when the object goes out of sight in the tunnel or screen conditions (e.g. 3, or 1 followed by 7), none is appropriate when the object is on either unoccluded section of the track (since all involve looking at some point other than the current position of the object) or when the object is passing over the platform. (Objection might be made to the use of the terms 'occluded', 'disappearance', 'reappearance', 'entry' and 'exit' in reference to condition 2, the platform condition. The results obtained, however, would seem to justify using the same terms for all three tracking tasks. Boundary occlusion, whether partial or total, produced very similar visual search behaviour in the infants tested here—see below).

Frame-by-frame analysis was also used to analyse behaviour on the stop trials. When the object stopped it was noted whether:

1. the infant's eyes stopped with the object, either remaining on the object for the entire duration of the stop or looking off at some point during the stop, or
2. tracked forward after the stop and, if so, whether immediately or after a pause on the stopped object, or
3. tracked backwards after the stop and, if so, whether immediately or after a pause on the stopped object, or
4. a combination of 2 and 3.

Behaviour on the rest of the stop trial, while noted, was not added to the tracking trials analysis as it was felt that the stop could well confuse subsequent tracking, making stop trials quite different in nature from the other trials.

From these measures we took two main summary measures, anticipation and confusion. Anticipation was defined as any track to the exit which occurred while the object was still on/behind/in the occluder and which incorporated a discernible pause at that point. Confusion was defined as above (looking at a location on the track where the object was not visible while the object was visible elsewhere).

Figure 4 presents the main results for anticipation in the three occluder conditions. It is obvious from Fig. 4 that the number of anticipations is not high at any week of testing, considering the number of infants and trials involved (12 infants × eight trials at each week) and the rather generous criterion for what was counted as an anticipation. If premature, unsuccessful anticipations had been excluded and only first trial anticipations counted (on the grounds that anticipation in subsequent trials could merely be reflecting increasingly skilful event prediction), the number of anticipations would have been very small indeed. Even so, it should be noted that any anticipation in the 'on' condition is not functional, since the object is continuously visible.

Confusion scores are presented in Figs 5A and 5B. On the identity theory, confusion represents the application of identity rules that are inappropriate to the presented physical reality. Application of rule 1 would produce place and/or movement errors. Application of rule 2 would generate increased attention to the occluder or to the other side of the track. Figure 5A, the confusion data from the three occluder tracking tasks, shows both the total number of inappropriate tracking responses and this total subdivided into the two different types of error. Two significant maxima are obvious and these were confirmed by mathematical regression analysis.* Figure 5B shows that even in the simple tracking task

---

* Newton–Spurrell coefficients were derived and from these the optimal regression curve was found by graphical means. This turned out to be a quartic curve of the form $c + ax^2 - bx^4$, a curve with two maxima which could account for 82 per cent of the variance in Fig. 5A.

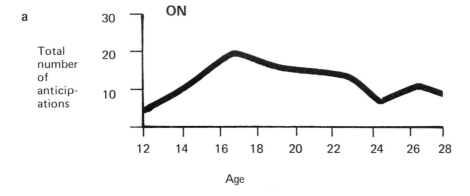

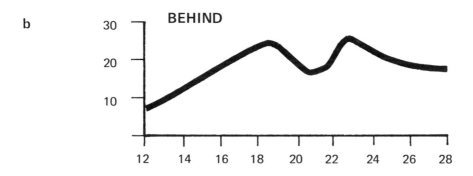

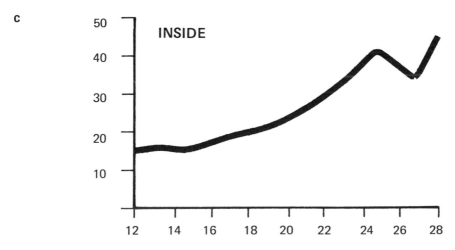

Figure 4. Total number of anticipations at each week of testing in the platform, screen and tunnel tracking tasks (number of subjects at each week = 12; number of trials for each subject = 8).

(no occlusion), infants who had previously tracked competently by the age of 14 weeks began to produce evidence of very confused tracking on a large number of trials.

We would argue that the two maxima in Fig. 5A represent successively peak testing of the rules that mark the first and the second advance, prior to their consolidation as reliable guides for search behaviour. To test the rule of the first advance—that an object is a bounded volume of space that can move from place to place—we would expect checking of locations where the object was not, since only one encounter with another object would be sufficient to invalidate the hypothesis, something that rigid attention to the object could never do. Similarly, testing the rule of the second advance—that an object is a bounded volume of space that can go into spatial relation with another object, both retaining their identity—would require both looking at empty places and checking out the platform, screen or tunnel. This is just what happens, the bulk of the second peak being accounted for by attention to the occluder. The first advance is thus occurring at around 17 weeks in this study, a result in accordance with others (Bower *et al.*, 1971; Bower & Paterson, 1973; Mundy-Castle & Anglin, 1973), with the second advance occurring at 22 weeks, well in advance of the age indicated by studies using other indicator behaviours (Uzgiris & Hunt, 1975; Wishart & Bower, 1984).

Unfortunately the results for the simple tracking showed a similar pattern of two maxima, both significant (Fig. 5B). The first maximum, reflecting the first advance, was wholly expected on an identity theory analysis; the second maximum, supposedly reflecting in Fig. 5A the testing of an hypothesis about identity and spatial relations, was not; there are no spatial relations for the baby to worry about in the simple tracking, hence there should, on identity theory, be no second maximum. Can we explain this second maximum in such a way as to preserve the putative significance of Fig. 5A? The only way we can see

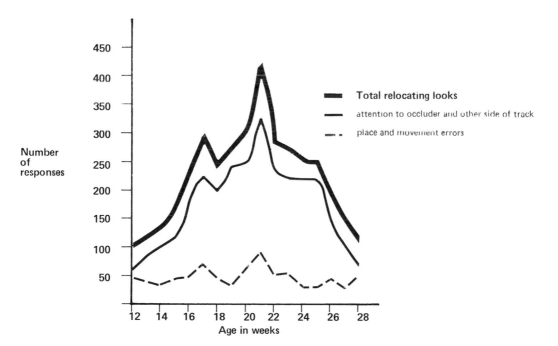

Figure 5A. Identity confusion in the three occluder tracking tasks. Confusion was defined as any track back or forward to some point on the track *other* than that at which the object was clearly visible. (Number of relocating looks were summed over subjects and the three conditions of occlusion for each week of testing; number of subjects at each week for each condition = 12.)

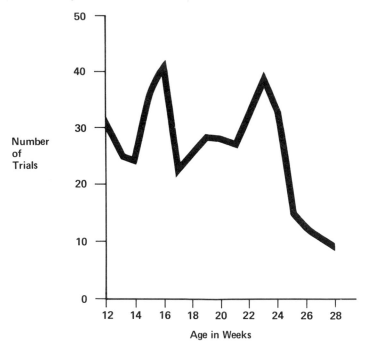

Figure 5B. Identity confusion in the simple unoccluded tracking task. Confusion was defined as in Fig. 5A—looking at a location on the track where the object was *not* visible while the object *was* visible elsewhere. [Number of trials on which confused tracking shown summed over subjects for each week of testing (max possible = 96 i.e. 12 subjects × 8 trials)].

to do so is to assert that the problems posed by the occluder situations transfer to the accompanying simple tracking situation. This could happen. The first advance results in a rule that is not a great simplification in the occluder situations. Application of that rule still results in perception of more than two objects (object and occluder) in these tracking situations. The gain in these occluder situations is minimal (Bower, 1982). The second peak of on-track but off-object looking in occluder situations reflects, we contend, checking to discover whether there are many separate identities to be seen on the track—as the first advance rule would predict—or indeed only one. Every time an object is not found, the result will undermine the general rule of the first advance, resulting eventually in the second advance. However, as that prior rule is undermined it will, presumably, be seen as a less and less reliable guide to action, even in the simple tracking situation, where it is quite adequate. In favour of this admittedly *ad hoc* explanation it can be said that such double peaks have not been found in studies where simple tracking was presented alone (Bower *et al.*, 1971; Harris *et al.*, 1974). In addition, the difference in ages of maxima between the simple and complex conditions favours the hypothesis. The first maximum in simple tracking precedes the first maximum in the occluder tasks which is what one would expect given that the discovery process should be more rapid in the simpler situation. The second maximum however is later, again what one would expect if it reflects the undermining of the rule of the first advance, undermining that can only take place in the complex situation.

   If this account of the visual tracking is accepted, it would seem that development of the object concept is proceeding apace in these babies. To discover whether these are genuine advances it is necessary to look at manual search behaviour. If these babies have made the second advance by 22 weeks they should be then in Piaget's Stage 5, conventionally measured by manual search.

Analysis: Reaching tasks

All three conditions were analysed in the same way. All behaviour was noted and divided into three time periods: behaviour prior to search, during removal of the occluder and during retrieval of the object. For each trial, time taken to remove the occluder was recorded and any delay between removal of the occluder and retrieval of the object noted.

In the cup and screen tasks, the criterion adopted for Stage 4 success was removal of the correct occluder within the two-minute time limit and recovery of the object within 10 seconds of its reappearance. In the case of the platform task, recovery of the object from the platform within the two-minute time limit was taken as successful Stage 4 behaviour. To be credited with being in Stage 5, all tasks required successful recovery of the object on all three (AAB) trials. Any attempt to remove or inspect the wrong occluder on the B trial was scored as a failure as was any trial on which the infant displayed surprise on reappearance of the object.

Table 1 shows the age of first presentation of the Stages 3–4 and 4–5 tasks and age of first success in these tasks for each subject. An infant was judged to have achieved a stage

Table 1. Age of achievement of Stages 4 and 5 in three different conditions of presentation

Subject	Platforms				Screens				Cups			
	First tested		Passed		First tested		Passed		First tested		Passed	
	4	5	4	5	4	5	4	5	4	5	4	5
1	19	20	19	20	19	19	19	19	20	21	21	21
2	17	18	18	18	17	20	20	21	16	18	16	18
3	17	18	18	18	18	19	19	19	17	19	19	21
4	19	24	24	24	19	26	26	27	20	24	24	24
5	17	19	17	19	19	20	20	(28)	18	20	20	21
6	18	21	21	21	18	20	20	22	19	21	21	21
7	15	17	15	17	16	21	20	21	19	20	20	20
8	25	25	25	26	25	28	28	28+	25	25	25	25
9	19	22	22	26	20	24	26	28+	19	27	27	28
10	15	18	18	18	15	19	19	19	16	21	21	21
11	18	22	22	22	19	23	23	24	18	21	21	21
12	17	23	23	23	19	22	22	24	18	22	22	23
13	18	21	21	(28)	20	26	26	(28+)	19	27	27	(27)
14	19	19	19	19	20	22	22	22	19	25	25	25
15	15	15	15	15	16	21	21	22	15	19	19	20
16	25	26	25	28+	25	—	28+	—	26	26	26	28+
17	15	17	17	20	18	28	23	(28)	15	21	21	21
18	20	21	20	21	21	21	21	25	20	20	22	22
19	18	21	18	22	20	20	20	25	19	21	21	24
20	17	17	17	17	17	19	19	19	17	17	17	17
21	16	21	21	21	16	21	21	28	17	23	23	23
22	21	21	21	22	21	25	25	25	22	22	24	24
23	19	19	19	19	19	19	19	19	20	24	24	24
24	18	18	18	18	19	21	22	25	18	18	18	18
Mean[a]			19·70	20·60			22·04	23·10			21·83	22·17
SD			2·83	3·23			2·94	3·24			2·98	2·85

*Ages in parentheses were omitted from calculation of the mean either because subject showed clear preference for the occluder rather than the object or because subject showed no interest whatsoever in that particular hiding task.

on that week in which he or she successfully dealt with one set of trials, with the proviso that:

no error was made if a second set of trials was presented in that session, or
if no second set of trials was presented in that session, no error was made on the next session in which that particular condition was presented.

As can be seen from Table 1, mean age of achievement of Stages 4 and 5 respectively was 19·70 weeks and 20·60 weeks for platforms, 22·04 and 23·10 weeks for screens and 21·83 and 22·17 weeks for cups. This fits well with the analysis of the tracking results forwarded in the preceding section. According to that analysis the transition from level 2 to level 3 identity rules occurred around 21 weeks in this group. Theoretically, this advance would allow these infants to cope with the object permanence tests that mark Stages 4 and 5.

Friedman two-way analyses of variance on age of achievement of Stages 4 and 5 for the three conditions showed that for both Stage 4 and Stage 5, age of success differed significantly in the different conditions ($4:Xr^2 = 14·25$; $5:Xr^2 = 21·84$—both significant at 0·001 level). Table 2 shows the results of sign tests carried out on age of achievement of Stages 4 and 5 in all possible pairs of conditions. As predicted, the platform task is clearly easier than both screen and cup tasks at both Stages 4 and 5. No difference was found between age of success on screen and cup tasks for Stage 4 but a significant difference in favour of cups was found for Stage 5, a finding which lends little support to any hypothesis that 'behind' holds a privileged position in the infant's understanding of spatial relations (Bower, 1974b; see also Lucas & Uzgiris, 1977).

Table 2. Results of sign tests on data in Table 1

Condition pair	Significance level (two-tailed)	
	4	5
Platform vs. screen	0·001	0·001
Screen vs. cup	n.s.	0·016
Platform vs. cup	0·004	0·004

What of the relationship (if any) between age of achievement of Stages 4 and 5? Stage 5, since it requires two successful A trials, cannot of course be tested until the infant has succeeded in the Stage 4 task. Inspection of the mean age of achievement of both stages for each condition shows that success on Stage 5 follows very quickly on Stage 4 success in all three conditions (Table 1). If, in addition, we compare age of achieving Stage 4 and Stage 5 in each baby and make allowance for the fact that the age of these babies often precluded presentation of both tasks in the same session (because of fatigue, irritability, etc.), it can be seen that, for platforms and cups, the majority of babies passed Stage 5 on the very first occasion of presentation (Table 3). If we include infants who passed Stage 5 on the second occasion of presentation, we see that, for screens too, Stage 5 success follows very rapidly on Stage 4 success. A trend analysis on performance over sessions confirmed the finding that there was no stepwise progression from Stage 4 to Stage 5, with 88 per cent of the variance being accounted for by a linear trend and no significant cubic trend being present. This fits well with the three-stage identity theory of the development of object understanding but poorly with the traditional six-stage interpretation of object concept development.

At 28 weeks, both groups of infants, E1 and E2, moved into further longitudinal object concept studies (see above) and continued to be monitored on the Stage 3–5 tasks at

Table 3. Relationship between age of achievement of Stage 5 and week of testing

	Platforms	Screens	Cups
No. infants achieving Stage 5 on first occasion of presentation	17/23	9/21	15/24
No. infants achieving Stage 5 on second presentation	4/23	6/21	6/24
Total	21/23	15/21	21/24

Note. Any infant in whom the gap between presentation and age of success was very large (e.g. infant 13: platform/ 7 weeks) but who had consistently shown clear preference for the occluder over the object throughout these weeks was omitted from this analysis—see Table 1.

regular intervals (monthly and fortnightly respectively). The Stage 5–6 transition task was also presented in these testing sessions. Criteria for success on all three transition tasks (3–4, 4 5 and 5–6) were the same: correct performance on all trials in two successive testing sessions, with age of success being calculated as age at the earlier of these two sessions.

As would have been expected from both the age and the earlier performance of these infants, no Stage 3–4 errors were found in the later testing sessions. The Stage 4–5 results from these sessions are more interesting, however, since it could have been suggested that the early passes on these tasks were not in fact true passes, infants only 'succeeding' because they were still too young to show the error characteristic of Stage 4 development. There were, however, only 11 errors found in a total of 864 presentations of the Stage 4–5 transition tasks in the later testing sessions. This makes it extremely unlikely that the successes in earlier sessions were false passes. If so, the normal Stage 4 errors would presumably have appeared in due course, at around 8 10 months. This did not happen.

Mean age of achievement of Stage 6 was also accelerated in both groups: 10·92 months in group E1 (SD: 1·24 months) and 12·45 months in group E2 (SD: 1·01 months).

Discussion

These results have numerous implications for theories of the object concept and for theories of infant cognition in general. Indeed, the most striking result, the massive acceleration in performance that was found, may have implications for general theories of development. The infants in these studies attained Piaget's Stage 5 by 5–6 months of age, and Piaget's Stage 6 by 11–13 months of age. In both cases, this is well ahead of both Piaget's longitudinal observations of achievement of this level of development and of more recently collected cross-sectional norms for this task. Wishart & Bower (1984) found that infants normally do not attain Stage 5 until 10 months, nor Stage 6 until around 2 years of age.

It is clear that the results found here lend more support to the three-advance hypothesis proposed by identity theory than to the more traditional five-step advance hypothesis derived from Piaget. Indeed one of the traditional and most researched steps, that from Piaget's Stage 4 to his Stage 5, in essence did not appear in this study. It did not appear at all in a large proportion of babies and was in no way a step-like transition for the remainder. Its attainment was rather the perfection of an existing skill, as shown by the smoothly linear nature of the change. Identity theory does not include the 4–5 transition as a necessary conceptual step but rather as a testing artifact reflecting one of several possible low-order techniques for coping with a situation that is not conceptually understood (see Bower, 1982; Luger *et al.*, 1984).

The suggestion that these infants were simply too young at testing to show the AAB error was ruled out by their performance over the following eight months of testing. The Wishart & Bower normative study mentioned above also demonstrated that infants in this age range can and do produce errors on this task. It could perhaps be argued that these infants did not show the AAB error because intensive longitudinal testing results in a different developmental sequence from that seen in cross-sectional studies. Another longitudinal study, done some time ago by the present authors, lends little support to such a suggestion however (Bower & Paterson, 1972). In this study, both experimental and control groups (the latter being tested regularly on object concept tasks but given no early tracking experience) produced AAB errors, the experimental group continuing to do so until 9 months on average, the control group until 11 months. This makes it unlikely that repeated testing on object concept tasks was in itself responsible for the non-appearance of Stage 4 errors in the present group of infants.

The hypothesis that there is a single developmental process underpinning the various behaviours seen to index changes in the object concept was also supported by the results of this study. As we have argued before (Bower & Paterson, 1972), acceleration is evidence of a *conceptual* link, if acceleration of one behaviour is produced by the exercise of another, completely different behaviour. In this case the visual tracking experience, in itself necessary for the first transition, surely made possible the accelerated attainment of the two other transitions. In this study, too, there was no evidence of *décalage* or repetition between eye and hand. Three advances in conceptual rules were sufficient to account for the changes in both visual and manual search. As for the two types of behaviour, one could claim that visual tracking permits a more sophisticated analysis of the conceptual rules in play; visual search is not restricted to two locations as is manual search, and therefore cannot misrepresent conceptual attainments in the way that manual search tasks, particularly one trial manual search tasks, can do (Bower & Paterson, 1972; Wishart & Bower, 1984). A purely visual search analysis of the third advance has not been attempted by us as yet; however, it would be simple enough to do so.

If there was no evidence of vertical *décalage,* there was sufficient evidence of between-task variation to indicate the possibility of horizontal *décalage* between in, on and behind. It seems likely that each of these relations poses its own specific problems that are mastered after the general problem of spatial relations has been tackled (see also Wishart & Bower, 1984).

The last sentence above proposes that in development it is the general, abstract problems posed by a task that are solved first, with attention to the task-specific details coming later. This kind of development theory (Bower, 1979) is not accepted universally. Many psychologists would prefer to see the baby constructing very specific little solutions that are gradually amalgamated into something more general. This latter hypothesis, while not directly tested here, was not supported here. The design ensured that on any week of testing of any one task the infants had had different numbers of exposures to that task. These differences were not reflected in performance. The observed performance on *one* task was a function of age and amount of exposure to any and all tasks, rather than amount of exposure to the specific task in question.

Lastly we should comment on the use of object concept tasks to assess intellectual development. They are widely used for this purpose (see e.g. Uzgiris & Hunt, 1975). It is also quite widely believed that these tasks predict later IQ (Birns & Golden, 1972; Wachs, 1975; Wishart, 1979). If this latter belief has any foundation, these results here have a more general significance, showing as they do that quite modest environmental manipulations can alter the rate of development in a very massive way.

Acknowledgements

This research was supported by MRC Project Grants nos. G972/982/C and G8314998N. We are also grateful to all of the mothers and infants who took part in this study and to Dr Rodney Noble for invaluable statistical help and advice.

References

Birns, B. & Golden, M. (1972). Prediction of intellectual performance at 3 years from infant tests and personality measures. *Merrill-Palmer Quarterly*, **18**, 53–58.

Bower, T. G. R. (1967). The development of object permanence. Some studies of existence constancy. *Perception and Psychophysics*, **2**, 74–76.

Bower, T. G. R. (1974a). Repetition in human development. *Merrill-Palmer Quarterly*, **20**, 303–318.

Bower, T. G. R. (1974b). *Development in Infancy*, 1st ed. San Francisco: Freeman.

Bower, T. G. R. (1979). *Human Development*. San Francisco: Freeman.

Bower, T. G. R. (1982). *Development in Infancy*, 2nd ed. San Francisco: Freeman.

Bower, T. G. R., Broughton, J. M. & Moore, M. K. (1971). The development of the object concept as manifested in changes in the tracking behaviour of infants between 7 and 20 weeks of age. *Journal of Experimental Child Psychology*, **11**, 182–193.

Bower, T. G. R. & Paterson, J. G. (1972). Stages in the development of the object concept. *Cognition*, **1**, 47–55.

Bower, T. G. R. & Paterson, J. G. (1973). The separation of place movement and object in the world of the infant. *Journal of Experimental Child Psychology*, **15**, 161–168.

Bower, T. G. R. & Wishart, J. G. (1973). The effects of motor skill on object permanence. *Cognition*, **1**, 165–171.

Bremner, J. G. (1978). Spatial errors made by infants: Inadequate spatial cues or evidence of egocentrism? *British Journal of Psychology*, **69**, 77–84.

Bresson, F. & de Schonen, S. (1977). A propos de la construction de l'espace et de l'objet: La prise d'un objet sur un support. *Bulletin de Psychologie*, **30**, 3–9.

Butterworth, G. E. (1977). Object disappearance and error in Piaget's Stage 4 task. *Journal of Experimental Child Psychology*, **23**, 391–401.

Gratch, G. & Landers, W. F. (1971). Stage 4 of Piaget's theory of infants' object concepts: A longitudinal study. *Child Development*, **42**, 359–372.

Gratch, G., Appel, K. J., Evans, W. F., Le Compte, G. K. & Wright, N. A. (1974). Piaget's Stage 4 object concept error: Evidence of forgetting or object conception? *Child Development*, **45**, 71–77.

Harris, P. L. (1984). The development of search. In P. Salapatek & L. B. Cohen (eds), *Handbook of Infant Perception*. New York: Academic Press (in press).

Harris, P. L., Cassel, T. Z. & Bamborough, P. (1974). Tracking by young infants. *British Journal of Psychology*, **65**, 345–349.

Lucas, T. C. & Uzgiris, I. C. (1977). Spatial factors in the development of the object concept. *Developmental Psychology*, **13**, 492–500.

Luger, G. F., Wishart, J. G. & Bower, T. G. R. (1984). Modelling the Stages of the identity theory of object concept development in infancy. *Perception*, **13**, 97–115.

Miller, D. J., Cohen, L. B. & Hill, K. T. (1970). A methodological investigation of Piaget's theory of object concept development in the sensori-motor period. *Journal of Experimental Child Psychology*, **9**, 59–85.

Mundy-Castle, A. C. & Anglin, J. (1973). Looking strategies in infants. In L. Stone, H. Smith & L. Murphy (eds), *The Competent Infant: Research and Commentary*. New York: Basic Books.

Neilson, I. E. (1977). A reinterpretation of the development of the object concept. Unpublished PhD thesis, University of Edinburgh.

Neilson, I. E. (1982). An alternative explanation of the infant's difficulty in the Stage 3, 4 and 5 object concept tasks. *Perception*, **11**, 577–588.

Piaget, J. (1936). *The Origins of Intelligence in Children*, London: Routledge & Kegan Paul, 1953 (original French edition, 1936).

Piaget, J. (1937). *The Construction of Reality in the Child*. London: Routledge & Kegan Paul, 1954 (original French edition, 1937).

Piaget, J. (1967). *Biologie et Connaissance*. Paris: Gallimard.

Uzgiris, I. & Hunt, J. (1975). *Assessment in Infancy: Ordinal Scales of Psychological Development*. Urbana, IL: Illinois University Press.

Wachs, T. D. (1975). Relation of infants' performance on Piaget scales between 12 and 24 months and their Stanford-Binet performance at 31 months. *Child Development*, **46**, 929–935.

Willatts, P. (1979). Adjustment of reaching to change in object position by young infants. *Child Development*, **50**, 911–913.

Wishart, J. G. (1979). The development of the object concept in infancy. Unpublished PhD thesis, University of Edinburgh.

Wishart, J. G. & Bower, T. G. R. (1982). The development of spatial understanding in infancy. *Journal of Experimental Child Psychology*, **33**, 363–385.

Wishart, J. G. & Bower, T. G. R. (1984). Spatial relations and the object concept: A normative study. In L. P. Lipsitt & C. K. Rovee-Collier (eds), *Advances in Infancy Research*, vol. 3. Norwood, NJ: Ablex.

Requests for reprints should be addressed to Jennifer G. Wishart, Department of Psychology, University of Edinburgh, 7 George Square, Edinburgh EH8 9JZ, Scotland.

T. G. R. Bower is also at the above address.

British Journal of Developmental Psychology (1985), **3**, 259–272   *Printed in Great Britain*

Adjustment of means–ends coordination and the representation of spatial relations in the production of search errors by infants

Peter Willatts

Three experiments are reported that examined infants' ability to use supports to retrieve objects that were visible or invisible, and covered or uncovered. Experiment 1* failed to confirm Frye's (1980) hypothesis that infants in Piaget's Stage 4 make search errors because they cannot adapt means–ends coordinations. Infants given a search task made errors, but infants presented with an uncovered toy on a support adapted to a change of support with few errors. Experiment 2 showed that infants did make errors with supports if the toy was under an opaque cover, and an explanation was sought in Butterworth's (1977) claim that errors are produced by covering the toy, regardless of its visibility. Experiment 3 confirmed this proposal by showing that errors still occurred on the support task if the toy was under a transparent cover. These results replicated Butterworth's findings, and are interpreted as supporting his code conflict hypothesis. In particular, it is argued that certain features of the no-cover support task help infants to coordinate egocentric and allocentric spatial codes and thus to avoid making errors.

Infants of approximately 7–12 months will search for a hidden object but often return to the original place of hiding when it is concealed elsewhere. These search errors were reported by Piaget (1955) who argued that they occur because infants do not represent objects as independent entities that can move from one place to another. Instead, objects are represented by the actions performed on them. The object hidden at place A is represented by the action sequence 'reach for cover at A in order to grasp object at A', and the object is just an extension of the action. This egocentrism on the part of the infant leads to repetition of search at A when the object is hidden at B. Only when the infant begins to represent objects independently of action does correct search at B occur, and the infant passes from Stage 4 of sensorimotor development to Stage 5.

A difficulty with Piaget's account arises from the interpretation of his concept of infant egocentrism. It is unclear whether search errors occur because the infant is egocentric with regard to the place of the object, or to the movement employed in retrieving it, or to both together. Recent studies have attempted to tease apart these components in order to identify the source of errors. Butterworth (1977) proposed that errors may derive from difficulties infants have in coding the position of the object. Position may be coded either by means of a self-related egocentric code, or one that focuses on the relations between the object and environmental features (allocentric code). The infant may use one type of code for the object's position and the other type for the cover. When the object is hidden at place B, only the allocentric code is altered and the egocentric code is left unchanged. The infant is then faced with a choice of places to search and makes errors.

The question of egocentrism with respect to the movement used to retrieve the object has received little experimental attention. The Stage 4 infant coordinates secondary schemes with the resultant separation of means from ends. The infant is able to perform one action with the intention of performing another, and Piaget noted many examples of means–ends behaviour which appeared at this time. In the case of search, the action of lifting the cover must be used before the object can be grasped. The infant may not properly understand this separation of means from ends, and could be uncertain about the appropriate means for retrieving the object when it is hidden at B. Errors would occur not because the infant

---

* Experiment 1 was reported in a paper presented at the Annual Conference of The British Psychological Society, University of Surrey, Guildford, 10 April 1981.

has failed to adapt the coding of the object's position, but because of a failure to adapt a means–ends coordination.

There is some support for this interpretation. Bremner & Bryant (1977) were able to show that infants persisted in repeating the same response even when moved from one side of the table to the other, regardless of the position of the object. However, as the authors themselves concluded, this does not rule out the possibility that infants did employ an egocentric code for the object's position. Better evidence comes from a study by Frye (1980). Following trials in which an object was hidden at A, 8- and 9-month-old infants were given an intervening task before the object was hidden at B. Infants who were distracted with a new object, or received a partial hiding task with the object previously hidden at A, or who received no intervening task all made search errors on B trials. Infants given a total hiding task at a new place (neither A nor B) made significantly fewer errors on B trials. Frye argued that the intervention of a means–ends task involving the object at a new place and separated from the original task eliminated the previous coordination at A. When infants later searched at B, the intervening task provided no source of conflict because it had been discarded, and the coordination at A had been deleted with the result that errors did not occur. The other interventions did not prevent errors because they did not involve means–ends tasks that could eliminate the coordination at A. In a second experiment, Frye extended this finding by using intervening means–ends tasks that did not involve search. Infants were given an object beyond reach but which could be retrieved either by pulling a cloth that supported the object or by pulling a string. The string intervention produced only a moderate reduction of errors and the most probable reason was that infants did not treat it as a means–ends task. It is doubtful whether string problems can be solved by infants as young as those in that study (Richardson, 1932; Uzgiris & Hunt, 1975). Infants receiving the intervening support task made significantly fewer errors on B trials, and the task was as effective as total hiding in eliminating errors.

Frye concluded that infants in Stage 4 experience difficulty in adapting coordinated sequences of actions involving means and ends. A search task with an object hidden at A and then B provides the condition in which adaptation does not occur and the result is an error. If Frye is correct, it should be possible to produce errors in other tasks that do not involve search but do require the infant to make a comparable adjustment to a means-ends coordination. Such a task should require the infant to retrieve an object by an indirect means from a choice of two alternatives (A and B), and for correct performance the infant should make an adjustment from using one means when the object is at A to the other when it is at B. Failure to demonstrate errors on such an alternative task would cast doubt on the generality of Frye's explanation, and would suggest that errors derive from some other aspect of the search task itself. Experiment 1 was conducted to discover whether or not Stage 4 infants are able to adapt means–ends behaviour in a task requiring the use of supports. One group of infants was given a standard search task, and a second group was given a support task in which an object was first placed on cloth A and then cloth B. It was predicted that errors would occur in both tasks when the object was at B.

Experiment 1

Method

Subjects.   The subjects were 48 infants of mean age 38·2 weeks; there were 18 boys and 30 girls. A further eight subjects were excluded for lack of interest or crying during testing. Parents of infants were contacted through notices placed in a local newspaper.

Apparatus.   Infants sat on their mother's lap at a table facing the experimenter. The table surface measured 122 × 60 cm and was covered with light grey Formica. Objects were presented on a flat sliding tray which measured 91 × 46 cm and was covered in the same material as the table. Two orange terry cloths measuring 20 × 30 cm served as covers or supports. They were placed on the tray 20 cm apart on either side of the midline with the narrow edge towards the infant. Several toys were used: a set of plastic beads, a squeaky plastic truck, a toy car and a wooden rattle which enclosed a bell. All trials were recorded on videotape by means of a camera concealed behind the experimenter.

Design. Subjects were assigned randomly to two groups. One group (search) was given a standard search task. A toy was hidden under a cloth at position A for five trials and then under cloth B for five trials. The other group (support) was presented with the object on top of cloth A, but out of reach. Five trials were given at A followed by five trials at B. On the A trials half the infants in each group received the toy at the left and half at the right.

Procedure. Infants sat with their mothers and played with the experimenter for 10 min in the testing room. When the infant had settled, it was carried by the mother to the table and sat on her lap. The two cloths were placed in front of the infant at the midline where they could be picked up and examined. The infant was then given a toy with which to play for about 20 s. If no interest was shown in the toy it was replaced by one of the others. After this familiarization with the materials, infants received four warm-up trials. A single cloth and the toy were presented at a midline position, and the infant was given two support trials and two search trials in random order. Warm-up trials were repeated if the infant failed to retrieve the toy, and different toys were used if there was an obvious lack of interest. Any infant who persistently failed on the warm-up trials was dropped from the study. Testing followed immediately. The two cloths were placed on the tray, one each side of the infant's midline, and about 2 cm from the edge of the tray. The toy was held up and when the infant looked it was either hidden under cloth A (search group) or placed on top of cloth A (support group). When hidden, the object was located under the centre of the cloth, but was situated at the far end of the cloth in the support condition. The procedure was repeated if the infant failed to watch the toy. After an interval of 3 s the tray was pushed forwards so that the ends of the cloths were about 12 cm from the infant's hands. The infant was allowed 30 s in which to retrieve the object, and about 10 s to play with it. If the infant did not retrieve the toy on a trial it was presented directly after the 30 s. The same toy was used on all test trials. Five trials at A and five trials at B were given in this way with an inter-trial interval of about 25 s. If the infant made an error and reached for the cloth which neither concealed nor supported the toy the tray was pulled back and correction of the error was prevented. The infant was still allowed 10 s play with the toy after making an error.

Video-recordings of all trials were viewed by the experimenter to identify which cloth was first pulled by the infant. In the case of infants who pulled both cloths, any interval of less than 0·5 s between successive pulls was counted as pulling both simultaneously. There were very few trials in which this happened. In addition, a record was made of trials in which the infant fixated both places before touching either cloth. It was thought that this measure might provide useful information about the way infants select which cloth to pull. As a check on reliability, a second observer who did not know the purpose of the study examined the recordings of five A or five B trials for 10 infants chosen at random from both groups. Agreement between the observers was 98 per cent for identity of cloth pulled first, and 96 per cent for fixation before contact.

Results

Errors on first A and first B trials. The number of infants producing errors or correct responses on the first A and first B trials is given in Table 1. There was no difference between groups on the first A trial ($\chi^2 = 0·67$, d.f. = 1), but the search group made significantly more errors on the first B trial ($\chi^2 = 3·88$, d.f. = 1, $P < 0·05$). Corrections were made for continuity, and infants pulling both cloths simultaneously were excluded. Changes in errors from the first A to the first B trial were examined with McNemar's tests. The search group made more errors on the first B trial ($P < 0·02$), but the support group showed no change. In the support group, more infants pulled the correct cloth than made errors on the first B trial (binomial $P < 0·01$), but the numbers in the search group did not differ significantly from chance.

Total errors on A and B trials. The mean total error scores for A and B trials are given in

Table 1. Number of infants in search and support groups pulling toy cloth or making an error on first A and B trials

Cloth pulled	First A trial		First B trial	
	Search	Support	Search	Support
Toy	21	18	11	17
Error	2	5	12	4

Table 2. Non-parametric tests were used for all analyses because there was a large proportion of zero scores. All tests were two-tailed. There was no difference in errors between groups on A trials (Mann–Whitney $U = 285$, d.f. $= 24, 24$, $z = 0.07$, n.s.) but the search group made more errors on B trials ($U = 146.5$, d.f. $= 24, 24$, $z = 3.02$, $P < 0.02$). Comparisons of error scores on A and B trials with Wilcoxon tests showed there was no change for the support group ($T = 49$, $n = 14$, n.s.), but the search group made more errors on B trials ($T = 18$, $n = 18$, $P < 0.002$). These results suggested an interaction between groups and trials with regard to errors. This was examined by comparing the change in errors from A to B trials between the two groups. A difference score for each subject was calculated by subtracting the total errors on A trials from the total errors on B trials. Comparison of these difference scores with a Mann–Whitney test indicated a greater increase in errors for the search group ($U = 184$, d.f. $= 24, 24$, $z = 2.19$, $P < 0.05$).

Table 2. Mean total scores for errors and fixation of both places prior to contact on A and B trials

	A trials		B trials	
Measure	Search	Support	Search	Support
Errors	0·75	0·71	2·33	0·83
Fixate both places	1·42	0·92	2·38	1·08

Persistence of error over B trials.   Infants did not perform randomly across the five B trials. In the search group, five infants consistently made no errors on the B trials, seven infants were consistent and made runs of from one to five errors from the first B trial, and 12 infants produced inconsistent patterns of errors and correct searches. This distribution of consistent and inconsistent patterns differed significantly from chance ($\chi^2 = 13.4$, d.f. $= 1$, $P < 0.001$) using a goodness-of-fit test, a finding that has been reported elsewhere for search (Butterworth, 1977; Butterworth *et al.*, 1982). In the support group, 13 infants made no errors on B trials, three infants produced runs of one to five errors, and eight produced inconsistent patterns. This distribution also differed significantly from chance ($\chi^2 = 33.09$, d.f. $= 1$, $P < 0.001$). In both groups, infants were consistent in their actions and tended to repeat their performance on the first B trial.

Fixation prior to contact.   The mean total scores for fixation of both places before any contact are also given in Table 2. Again, there was no difference between the groups on A trials ($U = 253$, d.f. $= 24, 24$, $z = 0.77$, n.s.), but the search group fixated both places more than the support group on B trials ($U = 174$, d.f. $= 24, 24$, $z = 2.43$, $P < 0.02$). The support group showed no change in fixation from A to B trials ($T = 56.5$, $n = 16$, n.s.) and the change for the search group did not quite reach significance on a two-tailed test ($T = 57$, $n = 20$, $P > 0.05$). Changes in fixation from A to B trials were compared between the groups, but the difference was not significant ($U = 229$, d.f. $= 24, 24$, $z = 1.23$, n.s.). However, fixation appeared to be related to the position of the object on A and B trials for the search group. Infants who received the object at the left on A trials and right on B trials did show a significant increase in fixation of both places on B trials ($T = 7$, $n = 10$, $P < 0.05$). Infants who received the object at the right on A trials and left on B trials did not show any change ($T = 26$, $n = 10$, n.s.).

Discussion

The majority of infants in the support group were able to retrieve the object by pulling the cloth. The change in position of the toy on B trials did not have the predicted effect, and infants adapted their performance with no increase in errors. In contrast, infants in the search group made many errors on B trials. This difference was apparent on the first B trial, and rules out the possibility that both groups produced errors but that the support group was able to adjust performance more rapidly across the five B trials. Differential rates of learning do not account for these findings.

The results for fixation show similar effects. Both groups fixated place A on the A trials before making contact with either of the cloths. On the B trials, infants in the support group switched their attention to place B, and showed little interest in the cloth that had previously supported the toy. The search group seemed more confused and often examined both places before reaching for a cloth. Although the search group did not show a significant change in the pattern of fixation from A to B trials, the reason for this was probably the unexpected position effect, and the likely cause was a sampling error despite the random allocation of subjects.

Although the support group appeared able to adjust a means–ends coordination, there are alternative explanations. Infants might have tried to reach directly for the toy, come into contact with the appropriate cloth, and pulled because it lay in the same direction as the toy and not because its role as a means was understood. However, this interpretation is unlikely to be correct. Field (1976, 1977) showed that infants markedly reduce attempts at reaching for objects that are beyond reach, so that behaviour which might have produced success does not occur. The distance of the toy from infants in the support group was 45 cm and was sufficient to eliminate attempts at direct reaching. In any case, this behaviour was rarely observed, and the cloths were grasped at the edge and not in the centre as the result of a failed reach for the toy. Richardson (1932) also found that attempts at direct reaching rarely occurred when infants were required to pull a string to retrieve an object that was 45 cm from the infant, and Willatts (1982) reported almost no attempts at direct reaching on other support tasks.

Another explanation is that infants did not distinguish the toy as separate from its support, but treated both as a unified whole (Piaget, 1955; Bower, 1977). Infants could have reached for the cloth supporting the toy because it appeared a more interesting object than the cloth that supported nothing. However, several studies of infants retrieving objects within reach and placed on supports have shown that the ability to treat both as separate (i.e. grasp the object and ignore the support) appears by 6 months (Bresson *et al.*, 1977; Wishart, 1979). Although young infants may regard an object on a support as a single object, infants in the support group were old enough to rule this out as an explanation for their performance.

Piaget (1953) did not believe that Stage 4 infants possessed the understanding of support that infants in Expt 1 appeared to demonstrate. He argued that, although the behaviour of pulling supports might be present in Stage 4, it was only through the operation of tertiary circular reactions in Stage 5 that knowledge of the support relation could be acquired. As evidence, he showed that his infants would still pull a cloth even when the object did not rest upon it, and this error did not disappear until Stage 5. However, Willatts (1984) proposed that Stage 4 infants may understand the relation of support but pull the cloth when the object is not on it merely from a wish to grasp something. In that study two tasks were presented to groups of 9-month-old infants. One group received a cloth that supported an object, and the other received the cloth with the object beside it, 5 cm from the edge. For both groups a low barrier was placed between the infant and the cloth that did not obstruct the infant's view of the object but prevented direct access to the cloth. The group with the object on the cloth removed the barrier, pulled the cloth and retrieved the object. The other group also picked up the barrier, but played with it, took far longer to reach for the cloth, and on many trials ignored it completely. The differences between the groups were determined by the spatial relation between the object and cloth, and it was apparent that 9-month-olds would not pull a cloth that did not support an object provided they had something else to hold. This finding lends weight to the claim that the support group was acting with an understanding of the function of supports.

The results of Expt 1 do not support Frye's proposal that Stage 4 infants are unable to modify coordinated actions in which means are separated from ends. This does not exclude the possibility that infants experience such a difficulty in the case of search alone, but we are left with the problem of identifying those features of the search task that prevent infants from displaying the competence shown in the use of supports. However, before proceeding to consider the particular difficulties that search presents, it is necessary to examine one difference between the search and support tasks.

The search group was presented with the toy under a cloth and within reaching distance. The support group was presented with the toy on top of a cloth and beyond reaching distance. Thus at the start of each trial the position of the toy varied in two ways depending on the group, and it is unclear whether position relative to the cloth (on or under) or distance from the infant was influential. It might be argued that infants found it easier to distinguish means from ends in the support task because only the means was within reach. The search task may have been more confusing because both means and ends were within reaching distance. Perceptual factors such as object colour do affect infants' capacity to identify means and ends (Bates *et al.*, 1980), and spatial factors may also be important.

One way of controlling for this is to present the search task as a modified support task. Experiment 2 was carried out to determine whether a search task that required the use of supports for retrieval of the toy might eliminate errors on B trials. Infants were first presented with a toy on top of a cloth, and the toy was then hidden beneath a cover. Infants searched by pulling the support in order to reveal the toy, and not by removing the cover. An experimental group received five A trials with the toy hidden on one cloth, followed by five B trials with the toy hidden on the other cloth. A control group received all 10 trials with the toy hidden on the same cloth.

Experiment 2

Method

Subjects.   A total of 48 infants took part with a mean age of 38·4 weeks; there were 21 boys and 27 girls. Another eight infants were excluded from the experiment for crying during testing or lack of interest.

Apparatus.   The same table and tray as in Expt 1 were used. The two orange cloths served as supports, and two extra cloths were used as covers. These were yellow, made of terry towelling, and measured 30 cm square. The set of toys was the same as before. All trials were recorded on videotape.

Design.   The subjects were assigned randomly to two groups. The experimental group was given a search task that involved the use of supports. Five trials were given with the toy supported on cloth A and covered with another cloth, followed by five trials with the toy covered on cloth B. The control group also received five trials with the toy supported on cloth A and covered, but these were followed by a further five trials at A. The distance of the toy from the infant was equal on all trials for both groups, and this was the same distance as for the support group in Expt 1. Half the infants in each group received the toy at the left on A trials, and half on the right.

Procedure.   Procedural details were similar to Expt 1, but differed with respect to placement of the cloths and toy. Infants were first allowed to handle the support and cover cloths and then a toy was found in which they were interested. Each infant received four warm-up trials in which a single support cloth was used with the toy. Two search and two support trials were given in random order in the centre of the tray. Following the warm-up trials, the support cloths were placed on the tray and their far ends hidden with the cover cloths which overlapped by about 15 cm. The toy was held up for the infant to see, one of the cover cloths was folded back, and the toy placed on the support cloth at the far end and covered. After a delay of 3 s the tray was pushed forward and the infant was allowed 30 s in which to retrieve the toy. In the meantime the experimenter kept both hands resting on the far edges of the covers. When the infant pulled the correct support cloth, the toy was brought forward and revealed, but the covers were retained by the experimenter. Previous pilot work had shown that allowing both toy and cover to be pulled on the supporting cloth was unsatisfactory. Depending on the strength of the pull, the cover could move with the support or be left behind. When an error occurred on any trial, the tray was withdrawn before the infant could reach for the correct cloth.

Video-recordings of all trials were viewed by the experimenter to identify which cloth was pulled and whether the infant fixated the support and cover cloths at both places before touching either support cloth. A second observer who was unaware of the purpose of the study scored five A or five B trials for 10 infants chosen at random. Agreement between observers was 100 per cent for cloth pulled first, and 90 per cent for fixation before contact.

Results

Errors on first A and first B trials. The number of infants making errors or correct pulls on the first A and B trials is shown in Table 3. The groups did not differ on the first A trial ($\chi^2 = 0.005$, d.f. $= 1$) but significantly more infants made errors on the first B trial in the experimental group ($\chi^2 = 5.11$, d.f. $= 1$, $P < 0.05$). A McNemar test showed that the increase in errors for the experimental group from the first A to the first B trial did not quite reach significance on a two-tailed test ($P = 0.058$ on a 3/11 split). The change for the control group did not differ from chance ($P > 0.1$ on a 3/2 split). More infants in the control group pulled the correct cloth than made an error on the first B trial (binomial $P < 0.002$), but the performance of the experimental group did not differ from chance.

Total errors on A and B trials. Mean total error scores for A and B trials are given in Table 4. Two-tailed Mann–Whitney tests showed that the groups did not differ on A trials ($U = 237$, d.f. $= 24, 24$, $z = 1.23$, n.s.) but that the experimental group made more errors on B trials ($U = 165$, d.f. $= 24, 24$, $z = 2.68$, $P < 0.02$). Examination of the change in errors from A to B trials with two-tailed Wilcoxon tests indicated no difference for the control group, but a significant increase for the experimental group ($T = 32.5$, $n = 19$, $P < 0.05$). Comparison of the difference scores confirmed the interaction between groups and trials. The experimental group showed a greater increase in errors than the control group across A and B trials ($U = 154$, d.f. $= 24, 24$, $z = 2.82$, $P < 0.02$).

Table 3. Number of infants in experimental and control groups pulling toy cloth or making an error on first A and B trials

Cloth pulled	First A trial		First B trial	
	Experimental	Control	Experimental	Control
Toy	19	19	11	20
Error	4	5	12	4

Table 4. Mean total scores for errors and fixation of both places prior to contact on A and B trials

Measure	A trials		B trials	
	Experimental	Control	Experimental	Control
Errors	0·58	0·83	2·08	0·88
Fixate both places	1·13	1·42	2·79	1·21

Persistence of error over B trials.   In the experimental group, five infants consistently made no errors on the B trials, nine infants were consistent with runs of one to five errors, and 10 infants produced inconsistent search patterns. The distribution of consistent and inconsistent patterns differed significantly from chance ($\chi^2 = 22\cdot15$, d.f. $= 1$, $P < 0\cdot001$). In the control group, 16 infants produced no errors on B trials, three infants had consistent runs, and five were inconsistent—a distribution that also differed from chance ($\chi^2 = 53\cdot6$, d.f. $= 1$, $P < 0\cdot001$).

Fixation prior to contact.   Mean total scores for fixation of both places are also included in Table 4. The difference between groups on A trials was not significant, but the experimental group fixated both places more on B trials ($U = 146\cdot5$, d.f. $= 24$, 24, $z = 3\cdot04$, $P < 0\cdot02$). The control group showed no change in fixation of both places from A to B trials, but the experimental group produced a significant increase ($T = 33\cdot5$, $n = 22$, $P < 0\cdot002$). The interaction between group and trials was examined by comparing the differences between fixation scores for A and B trials between the groups. The experimental group showed a significantly higher increase than the control group ($U = 126\cdot5$, d.f. $= 24$, 24, $z = 3\cdot37$, $P < 0\cdot002$). Significant increases were shown both by infants receiving the toy at the left on A trials ($T = 9\cdot5$, $n = 11$, $P < 0\cdot05$) and by infants receiving the toy at the right ($T = 8$, $n = 11$, $P < 0\cdot05$).

Discussion

Infants presented with a modified version of the search task made errors when the toy was moved but did not when it remained at the original place of hiding. The use of a support to retrieve the object instead of the removal of a cover did not eliminate errors. Inspection of the errors made by the search group of Expt 1 and the experimental group of Expt 2 reveals scores that are almost identical. It is unlikely that the group differences in Expt 1 were caused by differences in the distance of the toy from the infant or the method used to retrieve it. The experimental group also showed an increase in fixation of both places on B trials, but the effect of toy position on fixation reported for the search group in Expt 1 was not apparent. This reinforces the conclusion that such a position effect with the search group arose from a sampling error.

   This new method for presenting search problems involved considerable changes to standard procedure. The object was beyond reach while being hidden and when the infant searched, although the common procedure is to move it nearer for search. The covers were also beyond reach and could not be removed by the infant. Despite these changes, correct search on A trials and errors on B trials still occurred, so that direct action on the covers or the object is not essential for this to happen.

   It is difficult to see how a direct reaching explanation could account for infants pulling supporting cloths in Expt 2. It would have to be argued that infants were attempting to reach directly for a cloth that was beyond reach in order to obtain a toy that was not only beyond reach but was not visible. If infants markedly reduce attempts at direct reaching for visible objects that are too far away, it is even less likely that they would engage in such behaviour when the object was hidden. The 'unified object' explanation also appears implausible. Bower (1977, 1979) has argued that young infants' failure to understand the relation 'placed upon' is but one example of a general inability to comprehend spatial relations. Thus, one object placed on top of a support or under a cover loses its identity, and the infant regards it as amalgamating with the second object. The toy in Expt 2 was both on a support and under a cover at the same time, and would lose its identity in two ways. Although it is unclear exactly how the infant would regard this situation, it might be expected that the infant becomes even more uncertain of the whereabouts of the object, and would reach for either cloth at random. Bower (1979, p. 156) implies that this happens when the infant is faced with a choice of covers or supports, but that the infant quickly learns the rule 'to get the toy, go to *that* object'. However, the fact that the error rate on the first A trial was low, and remained so across further A trials, suggests that infants were not uncertain and did not need to acquire such a rule. Instead, this finding suggests that infants do show means–ends coordination in their use of supports.

Experiment 2 provided further evidence that search errors do not derive from a general inability to adapt means–ends coordinations. When errors were made it was clear that infants did not search as though the toy could only be found at its original location. Infants in the experimental group divided their search equally between the old and the new places. This was true both for the first B trial and across the remaining B trials. The control group showed no such pattern of divided search, but went almost exclusively to the original place. This division of search on B trials has been reported elsewhere (Butterworth, 1977), and, as Harris (1983) points out, poses a problem for any hypothesis which predicts that infants ought to search exclusively at the original place. Experiment 1 showed that infants adapted their performance on the support task, and Expt 2 showed that, when the toy in the support task was hidden, this adaptation only took place on about half the trials.

Hiding the toy involves two aspects: the toy is covered and is invisible. Either of these factors or both could be responsible for errors. In the support task the toy is uncovered and visible, and similarly either factor or both could be responsible for the lack of errors. One way of separating these possible contributory factors would be to test infants on the support task with the object placed under a transparent cover. If visibility leads to correct performance, then transparent covers should have no effect.

Butterworth (1977) found with a standard search task that errors were made when the toy was covered regardless of its visibility. He compared the performance of three groups: one was presented with an uncovered toy at A and B, a second group received the toy under transparent covers, and the third under opaque covers. The groups with covers made more errors than the group with the toy alone, and a visible toy only prevented errors if it was uncovered. Butterworth put forward the dual-code hypothesis to explain these effects. The no-cover group kept track of the toy because only an allocentric code was used, but the cover groups used egocentric and allocentric codes that produced conflict and errors. However, the different error rates between the no-cover and cover groups may have arisen, not only from differences in spatial codes, but also from differences between the tasks. Reaching for an uncovered object does not require a means–ends coordination, and Willatts (1979) has shown that infants do adjust their reaching to a change in an object's position by 5 months, several weeks before means–ends behaviour normally appears (Uzgiris & Hunt, 1975). The use of supports overcomes this difference between the conditions because a means–ends coordination is required to retrieve the object regardless of whether it is covered or not. Given this modification, the support condition of Expt 1 and experimental condition of Expt 2 are comparable to Butterworth's no-cover and opaque cover conditions. Experiment 3 was conducted to supply the third, transparent cover condition, and the aims were to replicate Butterworth's findings and to reveal whether the successful performance of the support group in Expt 1 was due to the object being visible and/or uncovered.

Experiment 3

Method

Subjects. A total of 24 infants with a mean age of 38·4 weeks took part; there were 13 boys and 11 girls. Another seven infants were excluded for crying or lack of interest.

Apparatus. The materials were the same as for Expt 2 except that the opaque cover cloths were replaced by transparent pieces of polythene, 30 cm square.

Procedure.   Exactly the same procedure was followed as in Expt 2. The infants were given five trials with the covered toy on one support cloth, followed by five more trials on the other support cloth. Half the infants received the toy first at the left and half at the right.

Results

For clarity, the infants in Expt 3 will be referred to as the transparent cover group, the support group of Expt 1 as the no-cover group, and the experimental group of Expt 2 as the opaque cover group.

Errors on first A and first B trials.   The number of infants making errors or correct pulls on the first A and first B trials is given for each group in Table 5. The groups did not differ on the first A trial ($\chi^2 = 0.23$, d.f. $= 2$), and comparison of scores on the first B trial also failed to show a significant difference overall ($\chi^2 = 5.33$, d.f. $= 2$, n.s.). Further pairwise comparisons between individual groups were therefore unwarranted. The change in errors from the first A trial to the first B trial for the transparent cover group also failed to reach significance on a McNemar test ($P = 0.34$ on a 3/7 split). Although more infants in the transparent cover group pulled the correct cloth than made errors on the first B trial, the difference did not differ significantly from chance on a two-tailed binomial test ($P = 0.15$). As reported above, the division of errors and correct searches on the first B trials was also at chance level for the opaque cover group, but the no-cover group made significantly more correct searches.

Table 5. Number of infants pulling toy cloth or making error on first A and first B trial

	First A trial			First B trial		
Cloth pulled	No-cover	Transparent	Opaque	No-cover	Transparent	Opaque
Toy	18	19	20	17	16	11
Error	5	4	4	4	8	12

Total errors on A and B trials.   Mean total errors on A and B trials are given in Table 6. The transparent cover group made significantly more errors on B trials than on A trials ($T = 25$, $n = 17$, $P < 0.02$). Overall differences in error scores between groups were examined with Kruskall–Wallis tests. There was no difference on A trials ($\chi^2 = 0.75$, d.f. $= 2$, n.s.) but groups did differ significantly on B trials ($\chi^2 = 6.11$, d.f. $= 2$, $P < 0.05$). Individual comparisons between groups were made with two-tailed Mann–Whitney tests. The no-cover group did not differ from the transparent cover group ($U = 208.5$, d.f. $= 24, 24$, $z = 1.7$, n.s.). The no-cover group made fewer errors than the opaque cover group ($U = 170.5$, d.f. $= 24, 24$, $z = 2.52$, $P < 0.02$), but there was no difference between the transparent cover and opaque cover groups. A Kruskall–Wallis test revealed a significant difference between groups overall in the change in errors from A to B trials ($\chi^2 = 8.43$, d.f. $= 2$, $P < 0.02$). Individual comparisons with Mann–Whitney tests showed that the opaque cover group produced a greater increase in errors from A trials to B trials than the no-cover group ($U = 149.5$, d.f. $= 24, 24$, $z = 2.92$, $P < 0.02$). The increase in errors for the transparent cover group did not differ significantly from either the no-cover or the opaque cover groups.

Persistence of errors over B trials.   Performance by the transparent cover group across B trials was not random. There were eight infants who consistently made no errors, six who made runs of from one to five errors, and 10 who produced inconsistent patterns of errors and correct searches. This distribution of consistent and inconsistent patterns differed significantly from chance ($\chi^2 = 22.15$, d.f. $= 1$, $P < 0.001$).

Table 6. Mean total scores for errors and fixation of both places prior to contact on A and B trials

	A trials			B trials		
	No-cover	Transparent	Opaque	No-cover	Transparent	Opaque
Errors	0·71	0·63	0·58	0·83	1·71	2·08
Fixate both places	0·92	1·42	1·13	1·08	2·29	2·79

Fixation prior to contact.   Mean total scores for fixation of both places before any contact of the cloths are given in Table 6. The transparent cover group fixated both places more on B trials than on A trials ($T=21$, $n=15$, $P<0.05$). There was no difference overall between groups on A trials ($\chi^2=2.41$, n.s.) but fixation scores did differ significantly on B trials ($\chi^2=12.27$, d.f. $=2$, $P<0.01$). Direct comparisons between individual groups for B trials showed that the no-cover group fixated both places less than the transparent cover group ($U=177$, d.f. $=24, 24$, $z=2.35$, $P<0.02$) and less than the opaque cover group ($U=124$, d.f. $=24, 24$, $z=3.47$, $P<0.002$). The difference between the transparent cover and opaque cover groups was not significant. The groups also differed overall on change in fixation scores from A to B trials ($\chi^2=8.61$, d.f. $=2$, $P<0.02$). Comparisons between individual groups revealed that the opaque cover group showed a greater increase in fixation of both places from A trials to B trials than did the no-cover group ($U=150$, d.f. $=24, 24$, $z=2.88$, $P<0.02$). Differences in the change in fixation between the opaque cover and transparent cover groups, and the transparent cover and no-cover groups, were not significant.

General discussion and conclusions

The present study essentially replicated Butterworth's findings. Infants made errors on the first B trial, and the differences between conditions were similar to the pattern that Butterworth (1977) described. Significantly more infants retrieved the toy than made errors when it was uncovered, but either an opaque or a transparent cover reduced the accuracy of search to chance levels. The analysis of total errors on B trials did not quite replicate Butterworth but the transparent cover condition was also of intermediate difficulty. It is possible that the sight of the toy beneath the transparent cover helped to distinguish the two locations; it has been shown that errors are reduced if the covers differ in appearance (Bremner, 1978; Cornell, 1979; Butterworth *et al.*, 1982).

The results for fixation did show clearly that it was covering and not invisibility that led to problems on B trials. On this measure the transparent cover group differed from the no-cover group as the latter rarely looked back to place A on the B trials, this suggested that adjustment of means–ends coordination and identification of the object occurred during placement of the toy on the support.

The accuracy of the no-cover group in comparison with the two cover groups does not support Frye's claim that Stage 4 infants are unable to modify a means–ends coordination and therefore make search errors. Infants in Piaget's Stage 4 do show means–ends coordination when using supports, and therefore the cause of errors must be something other than egocentrism with respect to response (see also Willatts, 1984).

These findings can be interpreted in the context of Butterworth's dual-coding hypothesis. Butterworth (1976, 1977) has argued that object identity is defined by spatial criteria, and that the code (egocentric or allocentric) determines the way this is achieved. Both codes are adequate for stationary objects, but only the allocentric code can be updated when an object moves. An infant using an allocentric code and perceiving objects against an invariant, external frame of reference could distinguish movement of the object from movement of the self to maintain object identity across changes in position. Evidence from studies of tracking skills (Bower & Paterson, 1973) and reaching skills (Willatts, 1979) indicates that the use of allocentric codes begins at least as early as 5 months.

The majority of infants in Butterworth's study who received a single, uncovered object at location B reached accurately. However, infants in both cover conditions showed a pattern of search divided between the A and B locations when the position of the object was changed. Butterworth proposed that the use of an allocentric code for the object and an egocentric code for the cover would account for the divided search if the two codes remained distinct and uncoordinated. The allocentric code might specify the object's location, while the egocentric code might specify the location of the cover for finding the object.

He offered two reasons for infants' use of such a dual-code strategy. Firstly, search requires the infant to retrieve the object by an indirect route, and the solution of detour problems may demand a spatial representation of this route. This ability may be limited or absent in Stage 4 infants. Secondly, the cover and object both occupy the same location, and this potential source of confusion may be overcome by the adoption of separate codes for the cover and the object. The performance of the no-cover group in this study showed that Stage 4 infants are able to solve detour problems, and that the spatial representation of the indirect route may not be beyond the capacity of the Stage 4 infant, at least for support problems. This conclusion is strengthened by the findings of Willatts (1982) who showed that 8-month-old infants rapidly and effectively adjusted their pulling of supports to retrieve objects that varied in distance from the infant.

The accuracy of the no-cover group may also call into question Butterworth's suggestion that dual codes are employed to cope with the difficulty of coding the positions of two objects occupying the same location. The position of the toy and the support did coincide, but the lack of errors indicates that an egocentric code for the support was not employed. However, it is possible that the support cloths were not perceived as objects in the same way as the covers. Instead, infants may have regarded the supports as backgrounds while the opaque and transparent cover cloths may have been perceived as objects because they were placed onto the background provided by the supports. Thus code conflict may not have arisen for the no-cover group because the supports, being part of the background, did not require an egocentric code. In addition, they might have enhanced the use of an allocentric code by adding structure to the invariant spatial framework. Secondly, infants may not have perceived the toy and support as occupying the same location. The toy was some distance from the infant, but the edge of the cloth was within reach; the consequence might be that allocentric codes could be used for both toy and support, so that conflict and errors would not arise.

A third reason concerns the availability of spatial information in the tasks, and the influence this may have had on coordinating spatial codes. Butterworth *et al.* (1982) have identified certain spatial conditions in which code conflict does not occur but it is unclear exactly why allocentric and egocentric codes should be dissociated in some situations and not in others. Examination of the task structures in the no-cover (support) and cover (search) conditions may provide a clue. Both tasks are similar; the infant must first achieve a subgoal before the main goal of grasping the toy may be achieved. However, the subgoals differ considerably. In the support task, the toy is too distant, and the subgoal to be achieved is that of changing the toy's position to bring it within reach. In the course of pulling the support, the relation 'toy-on-cloth' is maintained the whole time, and only destroyed after the main goal of grasping the toy has been achieved. In the search task, the toy may be within reach but cannot be grasped because the cover prevents direct access. The subgoal is to move the cover so that the toy is not under it, but the position of the toy is not altered. Achieving this subgoal destroys the relation 'toy-under-cloth' before the goal is achieved.

This difference in availability of the cloth–toy relation may affect the infant's coordination of egocentric and allocentric codes. Successful performance on the support task may occur because the infant can rapidly identify the correct cloth for achieving the goal. Even when an error is made, the relation toy-on-cloth is always present to provide guidance, and the infant can learn that to achieve the subgoal of moving the toy, the egocentric code for cloth A must be updated. Thus perception of these spatial relations encourages code coordination.

Less information may be available in search tasks when the object is covered. Once a cover is picked up, the relation that existed between it and the toy is no longer available. To understand why on some occasions search is successful and on others it is not, the infant must remember where the toy was located, which cloth it was under, and link that memory to success or failure. The coordination of egocentric and allocentric codes would be more difficult on a search task involving covers because the appropriate information about the relation between toy and cloth has to be remembered. Thus the act of solving a search problem eliminates some of the information that could assist in coordinating codes.

This implies that any other perceptual information that the infant could use to establish the relation between the toy and cover would do away with the need to rely entirely on memory, and would aid the coordination of codes. Some of the conditions studied by Butterworth *et al.* (1982) involving spatially distinct backgrounds or covers would appear to serve such a function as would the results of Freeman and his associates (Freeman *et al.*, 1980; Lloyd *et al.*, 1981). They found that search is more accurate if upright cups are used to hide the toy rather than inverted cups. This 'canonicality' effect is thought to derive from the infant's application of knowledge of containers to the problem of locating the cup which conceals the toy. However, as outlined above for support, the canonicality effect may have less to do with knowledge of cups than the ease with which an accurate representation of the toy's spatial relations is maintained. Butterworth & Jarrett (1982) have also noted that different perceptual information is available when a toy is hidden inside rather than under a cup, and that this may affect the production of errors. The analysis presented above for support could also explain why code conflict does not arise when a toy is placed inside a container.

The conclusion is that errors on certain search tasks are caused by difficulties in coordinating and updating the spatial relations that are commonly involved. The findings point to the need for a more careful investigation of the specific features of a task, and argue against placing undue emphasis on search for identifying the characteristics of any single stage of development. The use of support tasks provides an alternative method for examining the development of means–ends behaviour and infants' spatial knowledge.

Acknowledgements

The author thanks Liz Todd for assistance in scoring videotapes, and Anna Shewan, Aileen Sandilands, Margaret Grubb and Ian Rogers for secretarial and technical assistance.

References

Bates, E., Carlson-Luden, V. & Bretherton, I. (1980). Perceptual aspects of tool using in infancy. *Infant Behavior and Development*, **3**, 127–140.
Bower, T. G. R. (1977). *A Primer of Infant Development*. San Francisco: Freeman.
Bower, T. G. R. (1979). *Human Development*. San Francisco: Freeman.
Bower, T. G. R. & Paterson, J. G. (1973). The separation of place, movement and object in the world of the infant. *Journal of Experimental Child Psychology*, **15**, 161–168.

Bremner, J. G. (1978). Spatial errors made by infants: Inadequate spatial cues or evidence of egocentrism? *British Journal of Psychology*, **69**, 77–84.

Bremner, J. G. & Bryant, P. E. (1977). Place versus response as the basis of spatial errors made by young infants. *Journal of Experimental Child Psychology*, **23**, 162–171.

Bresson, F., Maury, L., Piéraut-Le Bonniec, G. & de Schonen, S. (1977). Organization and lateralization of reaching in infants: An instance of asymmetric functions in hands collaboration. *Neuropsychologia*, **15**, 311–320.

Butterworth, G. E. (1976). Perception and cognition: Where do we stand in the mid-seventies? In P. Williams & V. Varma (eds), *Piaget, Psychology and Education: Papers in Honour of Jean Piaget*. London: Hodder & Stoughton.

Butterworth, G. E. (1977). Object disappearance and error in Piaget's Stage IV task. *Journal of Experimental Child Psychology*, **23**, 391–401.

Butterworth, G. E. & Jarrett, N. (1982). Piaget's Stage 4 error: Background to the problem. *British Journal of Psychology*, **73**, 175–185.

Butterworth, G. E., Jarrett, N. & Hicks, L. (1982). Spatiotemporal identity in infancy: Perceptual competence or conceptual deficit? *Developmental Psychology*, **18**, 435–449.

Cornell, E. H. (1979). The effects of cue reliability on infants' manual search. *Journal of Experimental Child Psychology*, **28**, 81–91.

Field, J. (1976). The adjustment of reaching behavior to object distance in early infancy. *Child Development*, **47**, 304–308.

Field, J. (1977). Coordination of vision and prehension in young infants. *Child Development*, **48**, 97–103.

Freeman, N. H., Lloyd, S. & Sinha, C. G. (1980). Infant search tasks reveal early concepts of containment and canonical usage of objects. *Cognition*, **8**, 243–262.

Frye, D. (1980). Stages of development: The stage IV error. *Infant Behavior and Development*, **3**, 127–140.

Harris, P. L. (1983). Infant cognition. In M. M. Haith & J. J. Campos (eds), *Handbook of Child Psychology*, vol. 2, 4th ed. New York: Wiley.

Lloyd, S., Sinha, C. G. & Freeman, N. H. (1981). Spatial reference systems and the canonicality effect in infant search. *Journal of Experimental Child Psychology*, **32**, 1–10.

Piaget, J. (1953). *The Origin of Intelligence in the Child*. London: Routledge & Kegan Paul.

Piaget, J. (1955). *The Construction of Reality in the Child*. London: Routledge & Kegan Paul.

Richardson, H. M. (1932). The growth of adaptive behavior in infants: An experimental study at seven age levels. *Genetic Psychology Monographs*, **12**, 195–357.

Üzgiris, I. C. & Hunt, J. McV. (1975). *Assessment in Infancy*. Chicago, IL: University of Illinois Press.

Willatts, P. (1979). Adjustment of reaching to change in object position by young infants. *Child Development*, **50**, 911–913.

Willatts, P. (1982). Adjustment of means–ends coordination by 'Stage IV' infants on tasks involving the use of supports. Paper presented at the Annual Conference of the Developmental Section of The British Psychological Society, Durham, September.

Willatts, P. (1984). The Stage IV infant's solution of problems requiring the use of supports. *Infant Behavior and Development*, **7**, 125–134.

Wishart, J. (1979). The development of the object concept in infancy. Unpublished PhD thesis, University of Edinburgh.

Requests for reprints should be addressed to Peter Willatts, Department of Psychology, The University, Dundee DD1 4HN, Scotland, UK.

British Journal of Developmental Psychology (1985), **3**, 273–280   *Printed in Great Britain*

Hand–eye coordination and infants' construction of convexity and concavity

G. Piéraut-Le Bonniec

This study examined the development of visuo-motor coordination with respect to flatness and to concavity/convexity. The results showed that infants do not reach for objects with their hands differentially according to their concavity/convexity until well after they are able to distinguish these characteristics visually. Younger babies did not begin to adjust the shape of their hands prior to touching stimulus surfaces. By 10 months all the children modified their hand shape appropriately to the surface shape prior to contacting it. Convex objects were approached adaptively earlier in development than concave objects. During the 6–9 months period, the establishment of coordination between visual and haptic perception enabled the latter to supply the former with significant information.

Concave and convex objects are functionally complementary. The distinction between them forms the basis of the infant's construction of the logical and pragmatic relations of container and content. The aim of this study was to investigate the origin and development of the infant's recognition of concavity or convexity as opposed to flatness. This problem concerns the visual perception of three-dimensionality of space and also the recognition of an invariant object form.

Visual information allowing differentiation between flat, convex and concave objects is contained in differences in their optical texture, brilliance and shadowing (von Fieandt, 1949; Gibson, 1950; Yonas & Pick, 1975). Very young infants can differentiate between the presence and absence of gradients of texture density (Fantz, 1961; Bower, 1966; Fantz & Nevis, 1967) and between degrees of brilliance (Peeples & Teller, 1975); as a consequence investigations on the possibility of distinguishing concave from convex objects visually can be undertaken with infants only a few weeks old. In a previous experiment, Vurpillot & Piéraut-le Bonniec (in preparation) showed that 3-month-old babies do discriminate between a disc and a hemisphere and between concave and convex sides of this hemisphere. However, spatial relations can influence infants' behaviour at more than one level and information relative to the spatial properties of three-dimensional objects can be conveyed by two sensory modalities—touch and vision. The purpose of this study was to determine whether the visual discrimination of the objects presented in the previous study corresponds to a differentiated anticipation of the haptic properties of these objects as soon as the coordination of motor acts with visual information is established.

The spatial relation of concavity/convexity does not seem to have been the object of many experimental studies. Of those carried out, two studies used the method of cross-modal transfer between touch and vision. Bryant *et al.* (1972) and Ruff (1978) presented infants with three-dimensional objects which could be differentiated and identified by the presence of an indentation which has some similarity with a hollow or concavity. It appears from these studies that the spatial relationship of 'hollow in a three-dimensional object' is not abstracted and used by infants under 9 months of age either to categorize objects (Ruff, 1978) or to recognize visually an object they had previously touched (Bryant *et al.*, 1972).

However cross-modal transfer may not be the most appropriate paradigm to study infant capacity for distinguishing concavity from convexity. The anticipation paradigm could be more appropriate; several research projects attempting to demonstrate the existence of predictive capacities in infancy are based on the analysis of motor behaviour in the presence of a certain type of object that the baby may see. Thus the results of Bruner & Koslowski (1972) suggest that as early as 3 months babies can anticipate the type of activity which is appropriate to the object presented: feeling vs. touching. Experiments which have attempted to demonstrate the existence of depth perception used anticipation capacities on a 'visual cliff' (Gibson & Walk, 1960). More recently, Lockman & Ashmead (1983), Lockman *et al.* (1984) studied the development of anticipatory hand orientation with respect to horizontal and vertical orientation of a target, and found that 9-month-old infants demonstrated visuo-motor adjustments regarding object orientation to a greater extent than 5-month-olds did.

In order to determine whether visual discrimination between concave and convex objects leads to a differential manual approach, the anticipation paradigm was used. The question addressed was at what age is a three-dimensional object lying on a plane surface immediately perceived as a graspable thing and a hollow object as a container?

Method

Subjects

The subjects were 80 infants (42 males and 38 females): two 3-month-olds, six 4-month-olds, thirteen 5-month-olds, fifteen 6-month-olds, twelve 7-month-olds, thirteen 8-month-olds, ten 9-month-olds, four 10-month-olds and five 11-month-olds. Fourteen infants gave no response to the stimuli (eight 3-month-olds, four 4-month-olds and two 5-month-olds). The babies were in a day nursery in a Paris suburb and each was seen in a familiar room of this nursery. In addition, the infants were familiarized with the experimenters, who played with them and helped the staff feed the babies at meal-time. They were also familiarized with the operator and his camera.

Stimuli

Three rounded shapes, 8 cm in diameter, coloured dark green with lighter granulation, constituted the three stimuli F, V, X. Each one was located in the centre of a square board of 28 × 28 cm, painted light blue. F was a flat disc, V was a concave hemisphere receding from the back of the board, X was a convex hemisphere protruding from the board, towards the infant. Each stimulus was encircled by a white ring, painted on the board, 5 cm wide, its outer circumference having a diameter of 13 cm.

Procedure

The infants were placed on a small adjustable seat, arranged so that their backs were at an angle of about 100° to their legs. The baby was held with a belt which passed between the legs and around the waist. The arms and hands were completely free. The experimenter got on his knees in front of the baby, slightly sideways, and held out one of the wooden squares at the level of the baby's face out of reach; the surface of the square was at an angle of about 10° from the vertical to make stimulus identification easier. The object was presented in conditions of natural lighting: the subject's back was to the window and the objects received direct daylight. The baby's attention was attracted and when he or she looked at the object, it was slowly brought forward until it could be touched by the baby. The presentation lasted at most 30 seconds, beginning at the moment when the baby's attention was captured. The experimenter then changed the object and presented the next one under the same conditions. The objects were always presented in the order: flat—convex—concave—convex—concave—flat.

A total of 58 of the 80 observations were recorded on film with a 16mm Bolex cine-camera (24 frames per second). For the study of hand and finger movements, film recording provides clearer, more reliable pictures than video, as photos can be isolated from the film at regular intervals for comparison and classification, or shown to several people in case of doubt. However, due to the high cost of this type of recording, the other observations (22 out of 80) were recorded on a Sony videotape-recorder AV3440 (25 frames per second). Table 1 shows the age distribution of the infants who were filmed and those who were videotaped. In both cases the cameraman was 1·2m from the baby with the camera placed perpendicular to the baby and the experimenter, tilted slightly and filming slightly from above. The cameraman was instructed to focus on the baby's hand.

Table 1. Distribution of subjects according to age, pattern of response/no response and mode of data collection

		Age group (months)									
		3	4	5	6	7	8	9	10	11	Total
	$n=$	10	10	15	15	12	13	10	4	5	94
Subjects who gave a response to neither convex nor concave stimulus		8	4	2	–	–	–	–	–	–	14
Subjects who gave at least one response to both concave and convex stimuli		2	6	13	15	12	13	10	4	5	80
Mode of data collection											
Subjects who were filmed		2	4	10	10	10	10	8	2	2	58
Subjects who were videotape-recorded		–	2	3	5	2	3	2	2	3	22

Results

Analysis of recordings

First the films were analysed frame by frame and photos printed of those sequences concerning the approach of the hand, i.e. between the moment when the hand was about 10 cm from the stimulus (10 cm from the protruding portion for the convex stimulus, 10 cm from the square board for the flat and concave stimuli) and the moment it touched the object. Depending on the rapidity of the baby's movements (with older babies the movements are better controlled and less rapid) the number of frames corresponding to these film sequences varied from 8 to 18. A photographic sequence (see example in Fig. 1) was extracted from the film sequences. The video-recordings were also analysed frame by frame and the critical positions of the baby's hand photographed from the video at regular intervals. In this way, paradigmatic sequences were constituted enabling the classification to be made of the different types of approach recorded. Inter-observer reliabilities were 0·80 for classifying film sequences and corresponding photographic sequences. In the case of an ambiguous picture (20 per cent of the sequences), several naïve judges (at least three) were presented with photographic sequences, and a majority decision taken.

The different approaches

The sequences were analysed taking into account the following criteria at each stage of the approach:

(*a*) When the hand is about 10 cm from the stimulus: (*a1*) State of tonicity of the hand: is it flaccid or not? (*a2*) Position of the fingers: which fingers are folded back or bent and which are extended?

(*b*) When the hand is flush with the stimulus: (*b1*) Place of contact: is it on the blue part of the square board, or the white part, or the central part (disc or hemisphere), or the borderline, between the white part and the central part? (*b2*) State of the hand: is it flaccid or not? (*b3*) Position of the fingers: folded, or bent, or extended?

(*c*) When contact has been made and the hand is stable: has the shape of the hand changed in relation to its previous shape? An example is when the hand which was

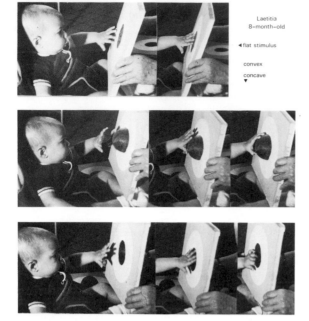

Figure 1. Example of film sequence: the approach with extended fingers. As can be seen, Laetitia (8-month-old) showed this type of approach for all three stimuli.

extended in (*b*) is closed in (*c*) (see Fig. 1); it was folded and has remained half-closed; the thumb and index finger being bent in a claw position have stayed on the object in this claw position.

The answers to these questions led us to distinguish between four types of approach.

1. The ballistic approach.   (*a*) The hand started abruptly from shoulder level and arrived in a state of non-tonicity, the fingers slightly folded. (*b*) It was flaccid and it pounced on a particular spot of the square board (possibly the central part). (*c*) The shape of the hand did not change but the hand did not remain at a particular place and moved over the surface of the stimulus.

2. The borderline approach.   (*a*) The hand arrived in a state of non-tonicity with fingers folded. (*b*) It touched the line of demarcation between the white and dark green parts of the stimulus; the part of the folded hand in contact with the object might have been the back or the palm. (*c*) The fingers stayed slightly folded during contact; occasionally there was a slight obtrusion of the index finger which came to touch the borderline precisely.

3. The approach with extended fingers.   (*a*) The hand arrived in a state of tonicity: it was extended, flat, fingers spread wide. (*b*) It came flat on to the central part of the stimulus. (*c*) The hand then adapted itself to this central part after contact was established; it closed round the convex stimulus, grasped the rim of the concave one, flattened out on the flat one, as seen in Fig. 1. The baby did not try to detach the convex hemisphere or to penetrate the concave one.

4. The 'adapted' approach.   (*a*) The hand arrived in a state of tonicity with the fingers prepared in advance for the object that it was going to touch: it was flat, with extended fingers if the stimulus was the flat one; the thumb and the index finger were bent in a claw position if the stimulus was the convex one and the hand was folded back if the stimulus was the concave one. (*b*) The thumb and the index finger touched the convex stimulus sideways in a grasping position and all the fingers closed up to penetrate the concave one. (*c*) The hand was in an adapted shape when it touched the stimulus and there was no change after contact was made.

The problem was to see to what extent the babies showed a differentiated manual approach when presented with a flat, a convex or a concave object. Each subject was therefore classified according to the pattern of his or her approach to each object. For example, one subject might be classified ballistic (flat), ballistic (convex), ballistic (concave); another might be classified extended fingers (flat), adapted (convex), borderline (concave). The pattern attributed to each subject was established from the first three presentations in the sequence flat—convex— concave and the rest of the sequence taken into account only when the baby did not respond to the first presentation (6 per cent) or when the behaviour in regard to it was not sufficiently clear (8 per cent). In this way two categories of subjects were established: those who had a differentiated manual approach and those who had a non-differentiated manual approach.

Table 2 shows that, up to the age of 8 months, 73 per cent of the babies belong to the second category whereas after 9 months they are all in the first. There is, however, a progression linked with age within these two categories.

Non-differentiated manual approaches.   The two 3-month-olds showed a ballistic approach for all three objects, as did 83 per cent of the 4 month-old babies; 69 per cent of the 5-month-old babies and 53 per cent of the 6-month-olds showed the borderline approach for all three stimuli; 58 per cent of the 7-month-olds and 69 per cent of the 8-month-olds showed an approach with extended fingers for all three stimuli (see Fig. 1).

Differentiated manual approaches.   From 8 months (23 per cent) and above all at 9 months (80 per cent) the babies showed the 'adapted' approach for the convex stimulus (i.e. in grasping position) but continued to approach the concave stimulus with the borderline approach or with the hand extended and just grasped the rim. The hand never penetrated

Table 2. Proportion of subjects producing each response pattern as a function of age

	Age group (months)								
	3	4	5	6	7	8	9	10	11
n^a =	2	6	13	15	12	13	10	4	5
Non-differentiated manual approach									
Ballistic approach to the three stimuli	1	0·83	0·30						
Borderline approach to the three stimuli		0·17	0·69	0·53	0·16				
Approach with extended fingers to the three stimuli				0·46	0·58	0·69			
		73 per cent of the babies up to age of 8 months							
Differentiated manual approach									
Grasping position to the convex stimulus					0·17	0·23	0·80		
Adapted approach to each stimulus					0·08	0·07	0·20	1	1
							100 per cent of the babies after 9 months		

a Total *n* = 80.

the concave stimuli directly. For the flat stimulus the babies used the approach with extended fingers. From 10 months, all the infants presented an approach to the flat, convex and concave stimuli which was not only differentiated but also adapted. With regard to the flat stimulus a new type of adapted behaviour was observed: the baby did not do anything, probably because the stimulus was uninteresting.

It must be noticed that the ballistic, the borderline and the extended fingers types of behaviour were observed all through the sequences (flat—convex—concave—convex—concave—flat) at 5, 6 and 7 months, as was the adapted approach to each stimulus at 10 and 11 months. Six babies did not show the same behaviour on both the first and second times. One 7-month-old and one 9-month-old penetrated the concave hemisphere the first time and grasped the rim the second time. Two 9-month-olds only penetrated the concave the second time. Two 8-month-olds showed grasping behaviour to the convex stimulus after they had approached it with extended fingers the first time.

Discussion

This study showed that the visual differentiation between relief and depth, which is apparent after 3 months, is not accompanied by an anticipation of the corresponding haptic properties. A differentiated approach to all three stimuli by all subjects was observed only after 9 months. One explanation for this could be that the infants perceived the potentially tangible properties of objects, but required more time to control the movements of their manual actions. A difficulty in motor control can be invoked to explain the fact that before 5–6 months the baby 'threw' his or her hand at the stimulus and that it fell on a random point of the object and sometimes the central point (ballistic approach). This can also explain the fact that, although after 5 months the hand was most often precisely directed to the borderline between the central part and the outer ring, the fingers did not grasp the object and were kept neither completely open nor completely closed. But 8-month-old babies could not only guide their hands towards a precise point; they could also tighten their fingers to enable them to be introduced into the hollow portion. It is well known that at this age they can grasp a small object. Thus, the observed delay in behaviour towards concavity cannot be explained by a simple difficulty in motor control.

Another type of explanation must be proposed. The present observations can be related to those of Campos *et al.* (1970), of Schwartz *et al.* (1973) and of Campos *et al.* (1978) who studied reactions to the visual cliff. These authors placed 2–9-month-old babies alternately on the shallow and deep sides. The 2-month-olds exhibited greater heart deceleration on the deep side, and that was interpreted as evidence that these infants discriminated between the two sides of the visual cliff but were not sensitive to the danger zone. In the case of 9-month-olds, there was heartbeat acceleration on the deep side, while the shallow side was still eliciting deceleration. If acceleration can be taken to be a reflection of a defence reflex (Graham & Clifton, 1966; Graham & Jackson, 1970), then perception of depth for 9-month-olds would imply an empty space, i.e. a spatial entity where one can fall. What was the meaning of the stimulus for the subject in the present experimental situation? One could say that, for the baby, the convex object is a graspable one before the concave object is a penetrable one or a container. While the babies who made an approach with extended fingers were only exploring or 'stroking' the protruding portion, the 9-month-old babies who showed an adapted approach for the convex stimulus (grasping position) also attempted to detach the protruding part (the second hand often coming to help the first to detach it). Nevertheless, these 9-month-old babies apparently still considered a concave object only as an object with a rim that can be grasped with the hand, as the 7- or 8-month-olds did; in fact, it might be thought that moving to the rim of a concave object is adaptive because this is a way of picking it up. However, the purpose of the older infants (after 11 months) seems different: they are more aware of or more intrigued by the containment function of concave objects. If one compares this experimental situation with the visual cliff, it could be said that the meaning of an empty space as a space which can be penetrated occurs later when the baby is presented with a concave object than when a space into which he or she can fall is presented.

Indeed it seems to us that the distinction between visual discrimination of spatial properties and knowledge of what they specify or mean is essential in the field of infant perception. But the problem is how does the infant manage to attach a meaning to what is perceived visually? We think that an intermodal elaboration of certain visuo-haptic properties is necessary to give this perception a functional value. From this point of view the period between 6 and 9 months seems to us to be of prime importance for perception and cognition of objects.

We have seen that it is during this period that the extended fingers approach is particularly important. In this type of behaviour it seems as if there is no anticipation before actual contact. But the baby's hand is open and stretched out as if in a state of alertness ready to adapt itself to the stimulus and gather information. Previously, in the ballistic and borderline types of approach, the baby directed the hand towards a place (the square board as a whole or the borders between shapes) but the hand was not ready to grasp full shapes. The knowledge of three-dimensional shapes as significant objects is rendered easier by the manipulation of the objects. Many objects are graspable and can be retrieved, thrown or banged. Perhaps concave objects are less useful for the baby even if, as Ruff (1980) emphasized, the experience of drinking milk from a specific cup makes it possible to detect in other cups and glasses the invariants specifying a container. Liquids and containers are differentiated both in terms of what happens to them—liquids are ingested, containers are not—and in terms of structural invariants which specify them—containers are rigid, liquids are not. But the container/contents relationship could be an asymmetrical one—contents coming from a container being an early experience, whereas the baby is less likely to fill a container.

The results obtained here seem to be consistent with the point of view of Gibson (1962), Zelazo (1976), Ruff (1978, 1980, 1982) and Bushnell (1982): the 6–9 month period is the period during which the establishment of coordination between visual and haptic perceptions enables the former to be supplied with significant information. Thus, even though the evidence shows that the perception of three dimensionality exists prior to this key period, the intermodal elaboration of certain visuo-haptic properties gives this perception a functional value.

Acknowledgements

The author wishes to thank M. Poizat for his assistance with data collection and the photo laboratory of the Maison des Sciences de l'Homme in Paris, for assistance in data processing. The author is grateful to E. Vurpillot for fruitful discussions and to the referees for their helpful comments on the previous draft.

References

Bower, T. G. R. (1966). The visual world of infants. *Scientific American*, **215** (6), 80–92.
Bruner, J. S. & Koslowski, B. (1972). Visually preadapted constituents of manipulatory action. *Perception*, **1**, 3–14.
Bryant, P. E., Jones, P., Claxton, V. & Perkins, G. H. (1972). Recognition of shapes across modalities by infants. *Nature*, **240**, 303–304.
Bushnell, E. W. (1982). Visual–tactual knowledge in 8–9½- and 11-month-old infants. *Infant Behavior and Development*, **5**, 63–75.

Campos, J. J., Hiatt, S., Ramsay, D., Henderson, C. & Svejda, M. (1978). The emergence of fear on the visual cliff. In M. Levis & L. Rosenblum (eds), *The Development of Affect*. New York: Plenum.

Campos, J. J., Langer, A. & Krowitz, A. (1970). Cardiac responses on the visual cliff in prelocomotor human infants. *Science*, **170**, 196–197.

Fantz, R. L. (1961). The origin of form perception. *Scientific American*, **204**, 66–72.

Fantz, R. L. & Nevis, S. (1967). The predictive value of changes in visual preferences in early infancy. In J. Hellmuth (ed.), *The Exceptional Infant*, vol. 1, pp. 351–413. Seattle: Straub & Hellmuth.

Gibson, E. J. & Walk, R. D. (1960). The 'visual cliff'. *Scientific American*, **202**, 64–71.

Gibson, J. J. (1950). *The Perception of the Visual World*. Boston; MA: Houghton Mifflin.

Gibson, J. J. (1962). Observations on active touch. *Psychological Review*, **69**, 477–491.

Graham, F. K. & Clifton, R. K. (1966). Heart-rate change as a component of the orienting response. *Psychological Bulletin*, **65**, 305–320.

Graham, F. K. & Jackson, J. C. (1970). Arousal systems and infant heart rate responses. In H. W. Reese & L. P. Lipsitt (eds), *Advances in Child Development and Behavior*, vol. 5. New York: Academic Press.

Lockman, J. J., Ashmead, D. H. (1983). Asynchronies in the development of manual behavior. In L. P. Lipsitt & C. K. Rovee-Collier (eds), *Advances in Infancy Research*, vol. 2. Norwood, NJ: Ablex.

Lockman, J. J., Ashmead, D. H. & Bushnell, E. W. (1984). The development of anticipatory hand orientation during infancy. *Journal of Experimental Child Psychology*, **37**(1), 176–186.

Peeples, D. R. & Teller, D. Y. (1975). Color vision and brightness discrimination in two-month-old human infants. *Science*, **189**, 1102–1103.

Ruff, H. A. (1978). Infant recognition of the invariant form of objects. *Child Development*, **49**(2), 293–306.

Ruff, H. A. (1980). The development of perception and recognition of object. *Child Development*, **51**, 981–992.

Ruff, H. A. (1982). Role of manipulation in infants' responses to invariant properties of objects. *Developmental Psychology*, **18**(5), 682–691.

Schwartz, A. N., Campos, J. J. & Baisel, E. S. (1973). The visual cliff: Cardiac and behavioral responses on the deep and shallow sides at five and nine months of age. *Journal of Experimental Child Psychology*, **15**, 89–99.

von Fieandt, L. (1949). Das phänomenologische Problem von Licht und Schatten. *Acta Psychologica*, **6**, 337–357.

Vurpillot, E. & Piéraut-Le Bonniec C. (in preparation). Visual perception of concavity and convexity by young infants.

Yonas, A. & Pick H. R. Jr (1975). An approach to the study of infant space perception. In L. B. Cohen & P. Salapatek (eds), *Infant Perception: From Sensation to Cognition*, vol. 2, pp. 3–31. New York: Academic Press.

Zelazo, P. R. (1976). From reflexive to instrumental behavior. In L. P. Lipsitt (ed.), *Developmental Psychology: The Significance of Infancy*. Hillsdale, NJ: Erlbaum.

Requests for reprints should be addressed to G. Piéraut-Le Bonniec, Laboratoire de Psychologie, 54 bld Raspail, 75270 Paris Cedex 06, France.

British Journal of Developmental Psychology (1985), **3**, 281–292   *Printed in Great Britain*

Failure to distinguish between people and things in early infancy

Benjamin Sylvester-Bradley

Whether or not babies understand the differences between people and things has been deemed crucial to psychological views of early development. However, only two studies have addressed this question empirically (Brazelton *et al.*, 1974; Frye *et al.*, 1983), neither of which reported statistically significant differences between the behaviours manifested by babies with a person and with a thing. Nevertheless, a number of psychologists assume in their theorizing that humans are born able to distinguish people from things (e.g. Trevarthen, 1974; Bruner, 1975). In this paper I describe a replication of the study reported by Brazelton *et al.* Eight 10-week-olds were filmed for two minutes *en face* with a graspable ball and 'chatting' with their mothers. Nine behaviours were coded. Results showed that babies opened their mouths and lowered their eyebrows significantly more and turned away significantly less with their mothers than with the ball. Further analysis showed that babies acted 'socially' in both conditions, suggesting that a 'sociable mood' may persist despite appropriate changes in infants' stimulus conditions. It is concluded that the ways in which infants experience their worlds cannot be generated by an inborn capacity to distinguish between people and things.

That the ability to distinguish people from things is considered crucial to human sociality by developmental psychologists can be illustrated in two ways. First, when psychologists deny that babies are social beings, they also deny that babies can distinguish people from things. Schaffer (1971) opens his influential book, *The Growth of Sociability*, with the statement that 'at birth an infant is essentially an asocial being'—a statement which he supports by claiming:

> Other people, he [i.e. the baby] soon finds out are fascinating things to watch and feel and listen to, but as yet they do not constitute a class of stimuli distinct from the inanimate world.

Alternatively, psychologists who claim that infants are social beings from birth claim, in their support, that infants do understand the difference between people and things. Thus Bruner (1975), in his article on the early development of communication, 'The ontogenesis of speech acts', supports his view that the child has an innate capacity to construct 'schemata for interpreting intersubjective phenomena' on the basis of 'ample' empirical evidence that:

> The child in his [or her] responses from a few weeks of age distinguishes the category of people from the category of things.

The evidence to which Bruner refers is a film study conducted by Trevarthen (1974) and Richards (1974) and reported at some length, although without numerical support, by Brazelton *et al.* (1974).

This paper reports my replication of the Trevarthen–Richards study and explores the difficulties of interpreting its results. My argument may at first seem paradoxical, for I report findings which show that there are significant differences in the behaviours which 10-week-olds manifest when facing a graspable ball or their mothers. Yet I submit that infants fail to distinguish between people and things in the manner claimed by Trevarthen, Brazelton and others. To conclude that babies are aware of the differences between people and things is, I believe, not only to contradict experimental and observational evidence of the type that I present but also seriously to misrepresent or gloss over the difficulties of understanding the complex ways in which babies experience their worlds.

What is the evidence *against* an innate ability to distinguish between people and things? Schaffer's case (Schaffer & Emerson, 1964; Schaffer, 1971) is based on both observational and deductive grounds. First, he points out that new-borns lack such social abilities as the discriminative use of vocalizations and the capacity for imitation. These observations can be seriously challenged, however; there is now evidence that babies as young as 4 weeks imitate oral and manual gestures (Maratos, 1973; Meltzoff & Moore, 1977). And, of course, while new-borns certainly do not have all the social abilities of adults they do possess a surprisingly large number that are relevant to social interaction: sensitivity to stimulation in all modalities, sensitivity to contingency (Papousek, 1969; Watson, 1972; Murray, 1980), an ability to coordinate their movements with those who are speaking to them (Condon & Sander, 1974), non-random facial expressions comparable in complexity to adult expressions (Oster, 1978), sensitivity to and control over gaze, varied vocalizations (Stechler & Carpenter, 1967; Pratt, 1977), pre-speech movements of the lips and tongue which resemble those of adults when speaking, and rudimentary gesticulations (Trevarthen & Hubley, 1978).

Second, even in cases where babies do treat people and things differently, Schaffer (1971, 1984) argues that their behaviour cannot be said to reflect an understanding of this difference until they can be shown to have certain cognitive abilities that are 'universally' recognized to underlie the distinction. For example, Kagan (1970) found that even very young babies spend more time looking at a human face than at any other naturally occurring stimulus. Schaffer argues that this is not because babies get involved in distinctively personal relationships with other human beings but because babies are pre-programmed to be attracted to the 'physical' stimulus properties which human beings happen to manifest. According to Schaffer, it should be possible to design a non-human *animated* stimulus that satisfies young babies as much or more than a person (i.e. by combining pattern, contrast, brightness, cuddliness, colour, rhythmicity, multimodality of stimulation, solidity, motility, etc., in an ideal way). He concludes that it is not until babies develop the concept of object permanence that they can begin to distinguish the qualities that make people different from complex physical objects (e.g. feeling and thought) and so become genuinely social beings.

It is important to stress that Schaffer's argument concerns the presence or absence of abilities in babies. He bypasses completely any questions about how babies experience their worlds. How, in the absence of an understanding of 'object permanence', do babies experience people and things? The negative definition of babies as 'asocial' beings tells us next to nothing about their positive qualities.

Schaffer's argument in the person–object debate has often been represented. For example, Lamb (1977) writes:

> There is near unanimity among theorists that infants are capable of [social] attachments only after they have developed cognitively to such an extent that they have an appreciation of the independent and permanent existence of others.

Such 'unanimity' can be traced back to the confluence of two theoretical currents in contemporary developmental psychology: Piaget's stage model of early development on the one hand and attachment theory (Bowlby, 1969; Ainsworth *et al.*, 1974) on the other.

Piaget (1947; Piaget & Inhelder, 1966) argued that social factors do not play a part in psychological development until the last quarter of the first year. Babies are considered profoundly egocentric, misapprehending the external world as a flux of continually changing images in which people appear merely as pictures amongst pictures. Only after acquiring the concept of 'permanent and independent existence' do babies begin to differentiate between their perceptions and distinguish the more enduring 'internal' qualities that make people different from other perceptual phenomena (i.e. subjective life, intentions, feelings, etc.).

Piaget's conclusions have been reinforced by attachment theory. Although attachment theorists claim that babies are born social, this initial social competence is conceptualized in terms of cybernetic 'control models' and inborn reflexes (for a critique of this view see Sylvester-Bradley, 1980). They do not deem babies to be *genuinely* social until about eight months of age when 'the first love relationship' is formed.

The idea that the first genuine sociability takes the form of a true love-relationship is most unsatisfactory. To accept it is not only to assume that babies love in a way which is not peculiar to babies but that young babies have nothing to compare with what, in adults, might be called *impermanent* social interests. Thus, on the one hand, adults have all those acquaintances who seldom if ever occupy their minds when are not in their company but who nevertheless take up a significant proportion of their social attention. It would also be a romantic idealization for adults to pretend that, when involved in intense sexual and emotional relationships, they have an unproblematic awareness of their counterparts' permanently independent existences, feelings and subjective lives. As I have suggested elsewhere, this type of idealization is characteristic of psychological thinking about the infant adult relationship. Psychologists promulgate an image of infancy which seems to reflect more the projection of the 'perfect romance' on to the first year of life than to reflect the exigencies of everyday existence (Sylvester-Bradley, 1983). Thus, both the claim that babies do not have a social life until they have mastered this 'cognitive' problem and the claim that they master it once and for all at 8 months of age and are thence 'genuinely social' seem too sweeping.

With respect to Piaget: of course, an understanding of the proposition 'X is a permanently existing entity' plays an important part in adult social life. But so do understandings of propositions like 'X is an informative entity', 'X is a comforting entity', 'X is a frustrating entity' and 'X is an amusing entity'. There is no logical reason why an understanding of permanent existence is necessary before babies can act and experience in accordance with these other propositions—though such action and experience may have reference only to what William James (1890) called 'the specious present'.

What is the evidence *for* an innate ability to distinguish between people and things? The best evidence has been provided by a group of researchers who worked with Bruner at Harvard in the late 1960s. Their evidence depends upon the claim that new-born babies:

> ... employ different modes of behaviour when relating to people or to things ... First observations indicate that when infants are given an interesting thing to look at they concentrate attention on it. The eyes narrow and scan over the object. The body posture seems tense. The arms, hands and fingers are oriented towards the object in incipient pointing gestures. With social situations the infant seems to 'sit back'. The body is loose and the hands and arms drop. The eyes widen and attention appears less focused. The face is more mobile with many mouth movements, and, of course, smiling is common (Richards, 1974).

Trevarthen (1973, 1979) has pushed this argument further by providing detailed descriptions of the wide range of apparently social behaviours that babies manifest in face-to-face 'conversations' with adults. In particular, he has described 'pre-speech' behaviour, delicate movements of the lips and tongue that closely resemble the lip opening, tightening, pursing, closing and lip and tongue oppositions essential to forming adult speech sounds. They are, he says, sometimes associated with rudimentary, speech-like breath control and often appear appropriately placed in the conversation-like exchanges he records between 2-month-olds and adults but which can also be observed from birth. Such 'pre-speech' is associated with a variety of communication-like gesticulatory behaviours and with complex displays of facial expression. Trevarthen contrasts 'pre-speech' with the 'pre-reaching' behaviours of very young babies—embryonic reach-and-grasp movements directed with a sober face towards objects—movements which, although rarely successful until the fourth month of life, are observable from birth onwards (White *et al.*, 1964; von Hofsten, 1979). Trevarthen concludes from these observations that babies are born with a faculty specifically adapted to the recognition and control of cooperative intentions and joint patterns of awareness—a faculty of 'intersubjectivity'—which contrasts with babies' faculty to act upon the inanimate world.

At first sight, Trevarthen's argument seems convincing but, while the importance of the behavioural modes which Trevarthen describes is not in doubt, their interpretation is open to question. It is perfectly possible for babies to manifest behaviours to which they do not attach the same significance as adult psychologists. And Trevarthen has published no formal evidence that babies:

> ... categorise unliving physical objects as different from living intelligent objects like their mothers and behave quite differently to these two kinds of thing (Trevarthen, 1974).

Both he and Richards do refer, however, to their filmed study contrasting young babies' behaviour to persons and to things.

The only published analysis of this study is by Brazelton *et al.* (1974). The films recorded the behaviour of five babies with their mothers and with a suspended graspable object at weekly intervals between the ages of 2 and 20 weeks. Brazelton *et al.* report that the:

> ... most striking observation was that there were two very different patterns of attentional behavior present early in each infant, which were called upon in response to an object versus a familiar person ... We felt that we could look at any segment of the infant's body and detect whether he [sic] was watching an object or interacting with his mother—so different was his attention, vocalising, smiling and motor behavior with the inanimate stimulus as opposed to the mother.

Despite the conviction of this statement, Brazelton *et al.*'s paper is not particularly conclusive. This is partly because the small number of subjects in the study precludes any statistically based generalizations. More importantly, none of the writers quoting this work seems to be aware of the difference between: (i) feeling *as scientists* that they, adult scientists, can consciously detect whether or not a baby is watching a ball or her mother's face, and (ii) knowing that *the baby* is aware of this difference and knows what it signifies. They thus commit what James (1890) called 'the psychologist's fallacy' by making 'the assumption that the mental state studied must be conscious of itself as the psychologist is conscious of it'. Similarly, Newson & Newson (1975) warn that 'behaviour, however complicated, carries no necessary implication that the organism is capable of appreciating the end towards which its own behaviour is directed'.

An attempt to replicate Brazelton *et al.*'s claim that 3-month-olds distinguish people from things has been reported by Frye *et al.* (1983). Their positive findings were that:

> Two groups of observers—parents and undergraduates—could judge from video-taped samples of 3- and 10-month-old infants' behaviour if the infants were alone or otherwise, with something that was active or passive, and if they were greeting or withdrawing.

But Frye and his colleagues found that lay-observers could *not* judge whether 12 3-month-olds were with an object or with their mother from one-minute film-clips of the babies in these two conditions. They were also unable to establish statistically significant differences between the rates of six behaviours occurring in the two conditions (hand to mouth; mouth open; cry; smile; look; arm move). However, as they themselves admit, different or subtler behavioural measures might have revealed such differences. On these grounds, I report below an attempt to replicate Brazelton *et al.*'s (1974) study using more refined categories of analysis.

Table 1. Incidence of each action in both conditions for each baby

| Type of action | Baby | | | | | | | | | | | | | | | | Mean | | Standard deviation | |
| | A | | B | | C | | D | | E | | F | | G | | H | | | | | |
	m	o	m	o	m	o	m	o	m	o	m	o	m	o	m	o	m	o	m	o
MO*	81	39	63	28	55	41	66	40	111	127	59	18	90	75	90	69	76·9	54·6	18·2	32·7
TP	24	4	1	2	11·1	9·7	12·1	3·7	14·2	28·2	4·8	4·2	25	24	24·6	24·3	14·6	12·5	8·6	10·3
S	6	0	0	0	0	0	1·2	0	2·8	1·2	1	0	0·9	0·7	0	1·3	1·5	0·8	1·9	1·0
ER	5	4	10	3·3	6·7	7·9	10·8	3·7	12·2	8·3	4·8	1·7	10·3	7·3	7·7	8·7	8·4	5·6	2·6	2·5
EL*	2	0	23	3·3	14·8	5·3	5·3	1·8	25·2	2·3	25·2	9·2	4·2	1·8	30·2	14·3	13·4	4·8	10·7	4·5
Y	0	1	0	0·8	0	1·8	0	0	0	1·2	0	0·8	1·8	0·8	0	1·2	0·2	1·0	0·6	0·5
TA*	3	5	0	0	2·7	3·2	0	0	0	1·2	3·9	6·8	6·0	7·3	4·7	5·7	3·0	3·7	2·0	2·8
R	2	3	18·5	12·5	4·6	3·9	1·3	1·8	11·6	15·2	2·9	3·2	5·2	4·3	5·7	4·2	6·5	6·0	5·4	4·6
DR	97	116	120	120	110·8	113·7	120	120	120	54·7	84·2	97·2	71·6	98·2	75·6	60	99·9	97·5	19·3	24·6

*Statistically significant differences between the 'mother' and 'object' conditions (Wilcoxon $P \leqslant 0.05$; two-tailed).

Note. All scores corrected to frequency per two minutes.

Key. Results: m = results for 'mother' condition; o = results for 'object' condition.

Actions: MO = mouth open; TP = tongue protrude; S = smile; ER = eyebrow raise; EL = eyebrow lower; Y = yawn; TA = turn away; R = reach; DR = duration regard.

Method

Eight mothers of babies aged 9–11 weeks (average age 10½ weeks) were contacted through their health visitors. After an initial home visit each mother brought their baby by taxi to the recording studio (University of Edinburgh) at a time when they thought their child most likely to be alert and active. Once the infants had been settled in their specially designed baby-chair [see Trevarthen (1977) for details], their behaviour was recorded in two conditions: with their mothers and with a stimulus to elicit 'pre-reaching' (see below).

In the 'mother' condition, the mother sat in a chair face to face with her infant at about 40 cm distance. She was asked to chat with and entertain her baby. This instruction gave rise to an animated facial display accompanied by a varied flow of baby talk. Mothers were instructed not to touch their children on the face or body in order that direct evidence of their presence did not appear on the video-recording during analysis of the infant's behaviour.

In the 'reaching' condition, the infants were confronted with a red wooden ball, 4·5 cms in diameter, moving slowly back and forth across their field of vision at distances varying between 15 and 40 cms whilst their mothers watched from an adjoining room. The ball dangled from a rod on a transparent nylon thread. The rod was held by the experimenter who stood as silently as possible behind the baby-chair. The ball was not moved evenly but in slow saccadic surges of 10–15 cms. 'Fishing' movements such as these are the most effective elicitors of 'pre-reaching' (Trevarthen, 1977).

For four infants (randomly preassigned) the 'mother' condition preceded the 'reaching' condition; for the other four, this order was reversed. Once a condition had started, approximately 2 min of behaviour was recorded, whatever that behaviour was. Since the infants were always alert and active at the beginning of the 2 min, the range of behaviours was limited—for example, no baby fell asleep during recording although some did grow drowsy towards the end. Neither did intense negativity occur (Sylvester-Bradley, 1981). So this, like most film studies of infant–adult exchanges (Sylvester-Bradley, 1983), was far from being a representative sample of infantile behaviour.

Nine categories of behaviour were coded: mouth opens (inter-observer reliability 0·85, coded MO), tongue protrudes (0·87, coded TP), smile (0·78, coded S), eyebrows raise (0·90, coded ER), eyebrows lower (0·80, coded EL), yawn (1·00, coded Y), reach (0·68, coded R), duration of looking (0·82, coded DR), incidence of turning away (0·93, coded TA). In order to maintain the 'blind' conditions of data analysis vocalization was not scored (if the sound had been turned on, the mother's baby talk would have been audible).

These behavioural categories were selected from Brazelton *et al.* (1974) and Trevarthen (1977) to best distinguish between 'communicating with people' and 'doing with objects'. Thus MO and TP were chosen to represent pre-speech; S, ER and EL to represent facial expressiveness, R to represent object-directed arm movements, DR and Y to express general level of interest, and TA to represent what Brazelton *et al.* (1974) call 'approach and withdrawal'. Brazelton *et al.* (1974) and Trevarthen (1977) indicate that object-directed activity is associated particularly with object-directed arm movements, intent visual regard of the object, a lack of facial expressiveness, and a lack of pre-speech. Communication is associated, on the other hand, with both facial and oral activity.

Results and discussion

The statistically significant differences shown in Table 1 suggest that 10-week-olds do behave differently in the two contrasted conditions—facing mother and facing an animated graspable ball. Infants opened their mouths and lowered their eyebrows significantly more and turned away less (took longer looks) with their mothers than with the ball. Each of these behaviours falls within what Trevarthen calls pre-speech or communicative action, suggesting a tendency towards oral activity, facial expressiveness and mutual gaze (the mothers looked almost continuously at their babies). Although the frequency of reaching was not significantly greater in the 'reaching' condition than in the 'communication' condition, there was a trend in that direction. These observations might be taken to support Trevarthen's and Brazelton's conclusions: that infants know the differences between people and things and tend to act accordingly in the appropriate conditions. However, I favour another hypothesis: that babies do manifest different modes of action, amongst which pre-speech and pre-reaching are two, but these are not adapted to what scientists or philosophers call the real world. They are a function of babies' *experience* of the world, experience which is *not* founded on innate knowledge of what to us are the differences between people and things.

Four assumptions underlie the Brazelton–Trevarthen conclusions:

(i) that the people–thing distinction is primary in the experience of infants;

(ii) that the infant's two most important modes of relating to the world are person-directed 'pre-speech' and object-directed 'pre-reaching' *behaviours* (Trevarthen, 1976) rather than different *moods*, as argued below;

(iii) that when there are no relevant transitions in the stimulus world, there will be no important transitions in the baby's mode of action; and

(iv) that whenever there is a substitution of person to object or object to person in the baby's stimulus world, there will be a corresponding transition in the mode of action manifested by the baby.

Observational and experimental work suggests a rather different orientation, based upon four considerations.

(i) The report of Frye *et al.* (1983) suggests that other dimensions of stimulation (alone vs. with an obvious stimulus; with an animate vs. an inanimate stimulus) produce a more telling effect on young infants than being with a person vs. being with an animated, graspable ball.

(ii) The results of Frye *et al.* (1983) also suggest that greeting and withdrawing are discriminable modes of action that occur with both people and things at 3 months. Moreover, as is usual in this type of experiment (e.g. Collis & Schaffer, 1975), inter-individual differences far outweighed inter-condition differences, suggesting that the claimed dichotomy of behavioural styles is not the best way of characterizing what goes on in these two situations. Finally, the results show that babies do not always appropriately change their mode of behaviour when a person is substituted for a thing or vice versa in their stimulus world. Thus all the behaviours that Brazelton and Trevarthen mention as supporting their claim, which I recorded in my study, occurred in *both* conditions for at least some of the babies. Babies reached at their mothers, for example, and smiled at the suspended ball. The significant differences I found were differences of frequency and not differences of kind.

The experiment described here showed that, when the data for both conditions were taken as a whole, and the subjects were ranked with respect to the frequency with which they performed the nine coded actions, mouth opening, tongue protrusion, smiling, eyebrow raising and, less significantly, yawning were found to be positively correlated with each other and negatively correlated with duration of regard and frequency of eyebrow lowering (Table 2). This positively correlated grouping might be called the manifestation of a 'sociable' mood. However, DR and EL did not form a second behaviour grouping in themselves—their coefficient of rank intercorrelation was only 0·07—so there were no obvious manifestations of 'concentrated attention' or a 'reaching' mood which complemented the 'sociable' mood.

Table 2. Rank order correlations between different actions for each baby taking the study as a whole

Infants' actions	S	TP	ER	Y	TA	R	DR	EL
MO	0·79	0·76	0·76	0·31	0·19	0·42	−0·64	−0·45
S		0·71	0·38	0·29	0·36	0·10	−0·57	−0·69
TP			0·72	0·79	0·57	0·10	−0·83	−0·30
ER				0·48	0·00	0·29	−0·50	−0·24
Y					0·62	0·10	0·48	−0·10
TA						−0·10	−0·24	0·10
R							−0·26	0·19
DR								0·07

Note. Spearman rank correlation coefficients with $P \leqslant 0.05$ in italic.

Further analysis suggested that the pattern of correlations in Table 2 arose because particular babies remained in a 'sociable' mood throughout *both* experimental conditions: that is, babies who raised their eyebrows, opened their mouths and stuck out their tongues most frequently at their mothers, tended to perform these actions most frequently with the ball also. Thus, when individuals are ranked in order of the frequency with which they performed the coded behaviours for the object and mother conditions separately, the order of ranks for MO, ER and TP intercorrelate positively with each other for the two conditions (see Table 3). Smiling in the object condition correlates significantly with MO and TP and (non-significantly) with ER in the mother condition but smiling in the mother condition does not correlate with these three behaviours in the object condition. This shows that babies who indulged in oral activity and eyebrow raising more often than their fellows with their mother also smiled at the ball more often than their fellows (but not vice versa).

Table 3. Correlation of the ranked frequencies of different actions in both conditions (for each baby) showing interpenetration of actions across conditions

Actions in mother condition	Actions in object condition								
	MO	TP	ER	S	Y	TA	R	DR	EL
MO	*0·74*	0·60	0·55	*0·81*	0·00	0·19	0·45	−0·50	−0·38
TP	*0·69*	0·60	*0·64*	*0·71*	0·21	0·57	0·05	−0·43	−0·36
ER	*0·67*	0·24	0·33	0·50	−0·31	−0·43	0·45	−0·07	−0·31
S	−0·07	−0·14	−0·29	0·05	−0·31	−0·12	−0·26	0·05	*−0·71*
Y	0·57	0·48	0·38	0·60	0·19	*0·67*	0·48	0·29	0·10
TA	0·07	0·36	0·17	0·45	0·21	*0·90*	0·07	−0·36	0·17
R	0·33	0·33	0·33	0·57	0·19	−0·19	*0·95*	−0·26	0·33
DR	−0·26	−0·55	−0·31	−0·48	−0·33	*−0·98*	−0·05	0·55	−0·10
EL	−0·33	−0·05	−0·10	0·19	0·10	0·10	0·02	−0·10	*0·90*

Note. Spearman rank correlation coefficients with $P \leqslant 0.05$ in italic.

These results disconfirm Brazelton *et al.*'s (1974) claim that one can look at any aspect of the infant's behaviour and tell whether he or she is in the company of a person or with an object. Babies act 'socially' in both situations, sometimes not being particularly influenced by person-to-object transitions. [Even when maximally different 100-second samples of 'object-adapted' and 'person-adapted' behaviours were sought in recording sessions lasting 40 minutes, the most contrasting sample recorded for any one baby showed that a number of 'social' behaviours occurred in both conditions, as did 'reaching' (Table 4).]

(iii) It is not difficult to observe transitions in babies' modes of action that have nothing to do with person–object transitions in their stimulus worlds. Thus, a baby may first manifest pre-speech and smile at an adult and then, for no obvious reason, reach for their nose or grasp their hair. Alternatively, a baby may first manifest negativity and then have their interest caught by a mother scratching her cheek or a particularly ingenious movement of the reaching ball by the experimenter (Newson & Newson, 1975) or be pacified by a sudden fascination with their own hand [see Sylvester-Bradley (1980, 1981) for described examples]. Such observations suggest that awareness of the person–object distinction is not primary from the baby's point of view and lead us to ask what are the factors that govern changes in the ways infants experience their worlds.

(iv) In a longitudinal study contrasting five infants' reactions to their mothers and familiar inanimate face-masks, what from the Trevarthen–Brazelton standpoint were 'inappropriate' transitions sometimes occurred on changing from mask to mother or vice

Table 4. Scores for one infant (aged 9 weeks) showing maximum differences between mother and object conditions

	Condition	
Type of action	Mother	Object
Mouth opens	38	7
Tongue protrudes	18	1
Smile	7	1
Eyebrows raise	8	3
Eyebrows lower	5	10
Yawns	0	0
Turn away	11	12
Reaches	19	18
Duration regard(s)	79·88	28·59
Vocalization	23	5

versa (Sylvester-Bradley, 1980, 1981, in preparation). For example, one baby smiled for a greater proportion (23 per cent) of one five-minute recording session with the familiar mask than she did in any of the 12 parallel sessions recorded with her mother (smiling max. = 19, $\bar{X}$ = 9 per cent) at fortnightly intervals during her first six months of life.

Conclusions

Following this discussion, how are we to assess the importance of the finding that, contrary to the results of Frye *et al.* (1983), there are significant differences between the ways that sub-3-month-olds behave with people and with graspable things? I believe we must say that the ways babies act are primarily a function of their different experiences of the world and their different moods. These moods are not based on a categorical knowledge of the differences between people and objects but can be affected in many different ways by the introduction or removal of people and things. In Table 1 we saw that the presence of a person can enhance the likelihood of babies performing certain facial and oral actions. Perhaps the mothers' own oral and facial activity evokes similar behaviour in their babies. Far from being proof of innate knowledge about people, such enhancement would fall within the category of what ethologists have called 'social facilitation'*:

> ... the performance of a pattern of behaviour already in the performer's repertoire, as a consequence of the performance of the same behaviour by other individuals (Hinde, 1970).

As Dunn (1977) suggests, such facilitation is unlikely to occur without a prior coincidence of calm, attentive, sociable moods in adult and infant. But once it occurs, once the child begins to appear to 'chat' with the adult, the well-documented propensity to interpret the actions of infants as meaningful will lead to a redoubling of the adult's conversational efforts (Newson & Newson, 1975; Shotter & Gregory, 1976). And if, as I argue elsewhere (Sylvester-Bradley, 1984), the primary structure of the child's relation to the world is narcissistic—in that babies originally gain pleasure from feeling that they create and control effects in the world that reflect their own actions—both baby and adult will be oriented in such a way that their responses gratifyingly amplify the other's reactions. The rewarding and seemingly conversational exchanges that result under such circumstances will in no sense be communications of intention but will nonetheless be crucial to the development of both the adult's and the infant's experiences of each other.

---

* Social facilitation is distinguished from 'imitation', which is a term reserved for more precise behavioural matching (Meltzoff & Moore, 1977; Sylvester-Bradley, 1984).

My attempt to explain the results of this experiment is deliberately schematic. Without methodical examination of infants' experience, we have little or no idea what part, if any, 'social facilitation' plays in the lives of babies. The concept of 'narcissism' also needs much refinement before it can help us to present a realistic picture of babies' initial preoccupations with their experience. My main argument here is that developmentalists do need concepts that make sense in terms of early experience. I merely point to social facilitation and narcissism in this context as likely to be more useful concepts than that of innate intersubjectivity.

In conclusion, to claim that babies are born with the ability correctly to categorize people as different from things is not simply to overestimate but to misrepresent both infants' *and* adults' relationships to their worlds. As Stout (1903) argued in discussing the growth of 'intersubjective intercourse', we owe the distinction between 'what is merely due to the varying conditions of cognitive process and what belongs to the nature of the external object' *to* cultural development and our involvement in social communion. The way in which we adults mark off inanimate things from the subjective order is itself a relatively late and fragile sophistication of human development. The person–object distinction is not the basis but a product of psychogenesis. By problematizing the nature of infants' experience of the world, I hope to have shown that there is no simple way of deducing that, because we can detect consistent differences in babies' behaviours with different stimuli, they experience those different stimuli as we do.

The difficulties of verbally characterizing infants' experiences, which are, by definition, non-verbal, are seldom discussed. Such difficulties are generally dealt with simply by selecting a few amongst many possible verbal labels when behaviours are recorded. But this method does not diminish interpretative ambiguity. The same infantile behaviours give rise to a whole host of incompatible descriptions in different studies. Thus, psychologists seem to find it possible to take any behaviour in babyhood as evidence for or against social competence depending on their theoretical interests. A survey of the relevant literature shows that all the behaviours coded in this study have been assigned different significances by different psychologists (Sylvester-Bradley, 1980). Even the smile, which one would think to be the social signal *par excellence*, is interpreted by Watson (1972) as an asocial response to the recognition of a fulfilled contingency expectation.

In this study, I have maintained that those who have built on a belief in babies' ability to differentiate between people and things a theory of innate intersubjectivity are mistaken. My results do not provide evidence for an inborn capacity to read others' intentions and to recognize some entities as intentional and others as inanimate. I have argued that proto-conversational exchanges between young infants and adults are better explained as the product of a characteristic coincidence of moods. I tentatively suggested that this coincidence might be maintained by the combination of three processes: the social facilitation of infants' behaviours by those of adults, the attribution of meaningful content to other-directed oral and facial activity in infants by their minders, and the process of primary narcissism which makes infants experience pleasure in seeming to create and control effects in the world which reflect their own actions. However, we will not know whether this explanation is correct until we find ways to describe not only infantile modes of action, but their *experiences* of the world—the existence, complexity and unpredictability of which I have stressed throughout this paper.

Acknowledgements

Thanks are due to those who have read versions of this paper or otherwise helped me with it: Margaret Donaldson, Judy Dunn, Fiona Grant, Norma Grieve, Martin Hughes, the late Margaret Manning, Martin Richards, Jane Selby, Colwyn Trevarthen and Cathy Urwin. They are not to blame for my views or my errors.

References

Ainsworth, M. D. S., Bell, S. M. & Stayton, D. J. (1974). Infant–mother attachment and social development: 'Socialisation' as a product of reciprocal responsiveness to signals. In M. P. M. Richards (ed.), *The Integration of a Child into a Social World*. Cambridge: Cambridge University Press.

Bowlby, J. (1969). *Attachment and Loss*, vol. 1, *Attachment*. London: Hogarth. (Also published by Penguin, 1971).

Brazelton, T. B., Koslowski, B. & Main, M. (1974). The origins of reciprocity: The early mother–infant interaction. In M. Lewis & L. A. Rosenblum (eds), *The Effect of the Infant on its Caregiver*. New York: Wiley.

Bruner, J. S. (1975). The ontogenesis of speech acts. *Journal of Child Language*, **2**, 1–19.

Collis, G. M. & Schaffer, H. R. (1975). Synchronisation of visual attention in mother–infant pairs. *Journal of Child Psychology and Psychiatry*, **4**, 315–320.

Condon, W. S. & Sander, L. W. (1974). Neonate movement is synchronised with adult speech: Interactional participation and language acquisition. *Science*, **183**, 99–101.

Dunn, J. (1977). *Distress and Comfort*. Glasgow: Open/Fontana Books.

Frye, D., Rawlings, P., Moore, C. & Myers, I. (1983). Object–person discrimination and communication at 3 and 10 months. *Developmental Psychology*, **19**, 303–309.

Hinde, R. A. (1970). *Animal Behavior*, 2nd ed. New York: McGraw-Hill.

James, W. (1890). *The Principles of Psychology*. New York: Holt.

Kagan, J. (1970). Attention and psychological change in the young child. *Science*, **70**, 826–832.

Lamb, M. E. (1977). Father–infant and mother–infant interaction in the first year of life. *Child Development*, **48**, 167–181.

Maratos, O. (1973). The origin and development of imitation in early infancy. PhD thesis, University of Geneva.

Meltzoff, A. N. & Moore, M. H. (1977). Imitation of facial and manual gestures by human neonates. *Science*, **198**, 75–78.

Murray, L. (1980). The sensitivities and expressive capacities of young infants in communication with their mothers. PhD thesis, University of Edinburgh.

Newson, J. & Newson, E. (1975). Intersubjectivity and the transmission of culture. *Bulletin of The British Psychological Society*, **28**, 437–446.

Oster, H. (1978). Facial expression and affect development. In M. Lewis & L. A. Rosenblum (eds), *The Development of Affect*. New York: Plenum.

Papousek, H. (1969). Individual variability in learned responses in human infants. In R. J. Robinson (ed.), *Brain and Early Behaviour: Development in Fetus and Infant*. New York: Academic Press.

Piaget, J. (1947). *The Psychology of Intelligence*. London: Routledge & Kegan Paul.

Piaget, J. & Inhelder, B. (1966). *The Psychology of the Child*. London: Routledge & Kegan Paul.

Pratt, C. (1977). A study of infant crying behaviour in the home environment during the first year of life. DPhil thesis, Wolfson College, Oxford University.

Richards, M. P. M. (1974). First steps in becoming social. In M. P. M. Richards (ed.), *The Integration of a Child into a Social World*. Cambridge: Cambridge University Press.

Schaffer, H. R. (1971). *The Growth of Sociability*. London: Penguin.

Schaffer, H. R. (1984). *The Child's Entry into a Social World*. London: Academic Press.

Schaffer, H. R. & Emerson, P. E. (1964). The development of social attachments in infancy. *Monographs of the Society for Research in Child Development*, **29** (no. 24).

Shotter, J. & Gregory, S. (1976). On first gaining the idea of oneself as a person. In R. Harré (ed.), *Life Sentences*. Chichester: Wiley.

Stechler, G. & Carpenter, G. (1967). A viewpoint on early affective development. In J. Hellmuth (ed.), *The Exceptional Infant*, vol. 1. Seattle: Special Child.

Stout, G. F. (1903). *The Groundwork of Psychology*. Manchester: Archive.

Sylvester-Bradley, B. (1980). A study of young infants as social beings. PhD thesis, University of Edinburgh.

Sylvester-Bradley, B. (1981). Negativity in early infant–adult exchanges and its developmental significance. In W. P. Robinson (ed.), *Communication in Development*. London: Academic Press.

Sylvester-Bradley, B. (1983). The neglect of hatefulness in psychological studies of early infancy. Unpublished manuscript, University of Cambridge.

Sylvester-Bradley, B. (1984). Narcissism and the myth of innate intersubjectivity. Paper presented at the BPS Developmental Section Conference, Lancaster, September.

Sylvester-Bradley, B. (in preparation). Changes in visual interest over the first six months of life: A longitudinal study. Child Care and Development Group, Free School Lane, Cambridge.

Trevarthen, C. B. (1973). Behavioural embryology. In E. Carterette & M. P. Friedman (eds), *Handbook of Perception*, vol. 3. New York: Academic Press.

Trevarthen, C. B. (1974). The psychobiology of speech development. In E. H. Lenneberg (ed.), *Language and Brain: Developmental Aspects* (Neurosciences Research Program Bulletin, vol. 12). Boston: Neurosciences Research Program.

Trevarthen, C. B. (1976). Basic patterns of psychogenetic change in infancy. Paper delivered to the OECD conference on 'Dips in Learning', St Paul de Vence, France.

Trevarthen, C. B. (1977). Descriptive analyses of infant communicative behavior. In H. B. Schaffer (ed.), *Studies in Mother–Infant Interaction*. New York: Academic Press.

Trevarthen, C. B. (1979). Communication and cooperation in early infancy: A description of primary intersubjectivity. In M. Bullowa (ed.), *Before Speech: The Beginning of Interpersonal Communication*. Cambridge: Cambridge University Press.

Trevarthen, C. B. & Hubley, P. A. (1978). Secondary intersubjectivity: Confidence, confiding and acts of meaning in the first year. In A. Lock (ed.), *Action, Gesture and Symbol: The Emergence of Language*. New York: Academic Press.

Von Hofsten, C. (1979). Development of visually-directed reaching: The approach phase. *Journal of Human Movement Studies, 5*, 160–178.

Watson, J. S. (1972). Smiling, cooing and 'the game'. *Merrill-Palmer Quarterly, 18*, 323–339.

White, B. L., Castle, P. & Held, R. (1964). Observations on the development of visually directed reaching. *Child Development, 35*, 349–364.

Requests for reprints should be addressed to B. Sylvester-Bradley, Department of Psychology, University of Melbourne, Parkville, Victoria 3052, Australia.

British Journal of Developmental Psychology (1985), **3**, 293–306   *Printed in Great Britain*   293 [85]
© 1985 The British Psychological Society

Developmental changes in four types of gesture in relation to acts and vocalizations from 10 to 21 months

Brenda Zinober and **Margaret Martlew**

The development of four types of gesture (instrumental, expressive, enactive and deictic) was examined in relation to acts and vocalizations in two infants over the period when they were aged 10 to 21 months. Observations were made in their homes when they were playing and reading books with their mothers. The initial predominance of acts declined while gestures increased from 10 to 18 months. The gestural types differed in their time of emergence, frequency of use and the context in which they were used. Generally, there was a progressive increase in the coordination of gestures and vocalizations but differences were found in when and how often gestural types were accompanied by vocalizations. These vocalizations showed developmental changes from babbling and proto-words to single and then multi-word utterances. Initially, co-occurring gesture and vocalization expressed the same meaning but as the two modes came to be used to express diverse meanings, more complex ideas were conveyed. During the period when the number and functional flexibility of the child's words are limited, gestures play an important role in enhancing communicative effectiveness. The establishment of an integrated, plurifunctional and increasingly conventional signalling system seems to provide a supportive framework for the acquisition of linguistic signals.

Children approach language learning with a well-established communicative repertoire based on skills developed in the preverbal period. Throughout infancy, mothers and their infants work together to achieve communicative goals. Mothers seem predisposed to provide supportive frameworks and predictable routines, initially taking a dominant, interpretative role in early interactions. They respond to, and build on, their children's biological propensities, progressively drawing their children into adopting conventional signals that will be accepted by the linguistic community to which they both belong (Lock, 1980).

By providing predictable routines and supportive frameworks, mothers encourage the development of a range of gestures that facilitate the growth of shared meaning. In the emergence of gestures, single forms of behaviour become integrated with other forms. Before the child acquires conventional linguistic signals, a variety of intentional and predictable gestural forms have been coordinated with eye-gaze and primitive vocalizations that function to convey a range of meanings in which gesture plays a predominant role. Changes in the form and function of gestures during the preverbal period are therefore important in themselves, providing insights into the communicative capabilities of the young infant. They are also of interest because of the putative relationship of gesture to emergent language skills with the suggestion of continuity between preverbal and verbal signalling (Bates *et al.*, 1975; Bruner, 1975; Bates *et al.*, 1979).

Gestures are formal movements whose primary function is to communicate meaning that can be interpreted consistently within a shared system. Intentionality differentiates them from signs, such as footprints or cries of pain. The *communicative* intention of gestures also differentiates them from acts. Acts are intentional movements, whose meaning can be interpreted by another person, but the intention of an act is directed towards an object or event, not towards a person (Zinober & Martlew, 1985). To signal interpretable meanings, gestures require the integration of several abilities: the voluntary control of movements forming the gesture, such as coordinated arm and hand control, that are eventually integrated with gaze and vocalization; the intention to convey particular signals in given contexts; the approximation to socially accepted forms, recognizable within a shared system; and reciprocity in interpretation. Over the first year there is increasing elaboration and integration of these skills. Initially infants use whatever movements are available, responding to different situations with a limited set of signals. Then they develop appropriate differentiated responses that are goal-corrected for the specific context (Kaye, 1982).

Intentional gestures probably have origins in earlier forms of behaviour, whose initial function may differ from later manifestations of the behaviour (Trevarthen, 1979; Fogel, 1981; Thelen, 1981; Lockman & Ashmead, 1983). Many movement forms appear before the age when they seem necessary or functionally significant—for example, the primary walking of neonates, or index finger pointing in the first month. In the emergence of intentional gestures, parents interpret, and therefore respond in a reinforcing manner, both to those gestures that show fairly close approximations to conventional signals and to those of a more idiosyncratic nature which eventually die out. These are interpreted from contextual cues, thus facilitating the development of preadaptive mechanisms. R. A. Clark (1978), for instance, suggests that mothers play an essential part in interpreting and conventionalizing the social interchange which involves the exchange of objects. The reaching gesture emerges from the act because eventually it is not used simply to get an object but to produce a change in the mother's behaviour.

Gestures serve a variety of functions, though most interest in infants' gestures has centred on instrumental and deictic expressions. In our investigations, we extended this range to include all the gestures we observed being used by the children we studied. We categorized these into four functions, adapted from an original taxonomy suggested by Barten (1977). These cover the communication of emotional states and reactions (expressive), the intention to get things done or regulate another's behaviour (instrumental), symbols created to represent events to engage in shared exchanges (enactive) and indicating a focus of shared interest (deictic). Categorizing function in these ways takes account of the specific contexts of infancy that encourage the development of shared meaning and possible relations with language acquisition.

Instrumental gestures function to get services performed or to control another's behaviour. They seem to have their origins in acts that are, at first, only unintentionally communicative. For instance, the reaching gesture with the opening and shutting fist to request an object can be seen as emerging from the act of reaching out for and grasping an object (R. A. Clark, 1978). Instrumental reaching has been observed to give way to pointing by Leung & Rheingold (1981). Although reaching emerges before pointing, they are both coordinated with eye-gaze and conventional vocalization at about the same time (Masur, 1983).

Expressive gestures seem to derive from early behaviours, such as rhythmic movements, that come under voluntary control and become stylized. Arm and leg waving, for instance, seen in the first year, become intentionally communicative when the movements are used systematically and are coordinated with eye-gaze and possibly vocalization (for example, arm flapping as a consistent response to an offered treat). Similarly, smiling can qualify as an expressive gesture, when combined with deliberate head orientation, mutual eye-gaze and shared focus of attention as an intentional signal of pleasure in an event. Although expressive gesture can be idiosyncratic, and often not used reciprocally by the mother, they are easily interpretable within the shared system of the mother/child dyad and usually beyond this.

Enactive gestures differ from the other gestures we examined in that they synthesize the attributes of events, formalizing them to signify meaning. They occur principally in the context of pretend play and enacting events in finger rhymes. Bates *et al.* (1977, 1980) have referred to them as 'symbolic gestures' and Escalona (1973) as 'enactive naming'. These gestures can arise out of technical acts (for example, imitating the turning of a door handle) but generally they are acquired through imitation and modelling (for example, the actions accompanying rhyming games).

Deictic gestures serve to focus joint attention on an object or event. They could be showing an object in an open hand or pointing. Of all gestural forms, pointing has received most attention. We define pointing as a manual gesture involving index finger extension in which the finger may or may not touch the referent. As a mature gesture, this is accompanied by a verbal comment and visual monitoring to check that the person addressed is attending and following. Bates *et al.* (1979) found that communicative points, that is points which involved some coordinated attempt to check for adult confirmation, were the strongest predictors of language development of all the gestures they observed.

Masur (1983) traced the emergence and development of three object-related gestures: pointing, extending objects and open-handed reaching in infants aged 9–18 months. Pointing was the last of these gestures to emerge at around 12–14 months. When behaviours were coordinated with dual directional signalling, this appeared concurrently across all types of gestures; for example, the infant looked from object to mother when the object was not in the same visual field to request or to convey interest in the object. Only after dual directional signalling had appeared at about 13 months were words used in conjunction with gestures.

Increasing complexity in coordination of communicative signals was noted also by Murphy (1978). She observed pointing gestures in groups of infants aged 9, 14, 20 and 24 months who were looking at books. She found that pointing emerged at 9 months but was not integrated with vocal activity until 14 months. By 20 months pointing was well established. It could be used in successive strings and also labelling was well synchronized with gesture. Visual regard of the mother was generally absent as these observations were made solely in a book-reading context. Murphy suggests that children omit communicative gaze when they assume their mother's attention can be taken for granted.

The above four types of gesture formed the basis of our investigation into the development of intentional signalling, and were looked at in relation to acts and vocalizations. In the period from 10 to 21 months, the infant is relying less on parents having to make inferences about possible meanings. During the first year, for instance, children act directly upon objects while mothers impute meaning from their childrens' behaviour. From about 9–10 months, certain non-communicative acts begin to be replaced by intentional gestures. We therefore included acts in our analyses to trace predicted trends in the decline of acts as gestures increased.

We were also interested in examining the emergence of vocalization and its coordination with the various types of gesture. Following the period of reduplicated babbling which is essentially non-communicative (Stark, 1979), children have been found to use a transitional form of vocalization that both precedes and runs concurrently with the production of conventional single-word utterances (Dore *et al.*, 1976; Ferguson, 1976). These proto-words are utterances whose forms are derived from babbling but are not targeted on the adult representation of language. They fulfil limited communicative functions: expressing likes and dislikes; wanting and rejecting; sharing of interest and indicating. The use of gesture in relation to these transitional phenomena and to conventional words was examined as part of our investigation into the increasing coordination and complexity of gestural signals.

Children's acquisition of linguistic functions shows that initially they are only able to use words to express a single function before they can use them in a plurifunctional manner (Halliday, 1975). We categorized gestures as having a primary function but expected that children would develop the ability to use gestures belonging primarily or intially to one category to function eventually for an additional purpose. For example, pointing, initially used to indicate an object which the child finds interesting, could come to be used to request an object.

Method

Subjects

Observations were made of two children, Adam and William, interacting with their mothers. The study covered the period when the children were aged 10 to 21 months. Both mothers were teachers and were contacted through the National Childbirth Trust.

Observations

Eight observations were made in the homes of the children at approximately six-weekly intervals. There were slight differences in the children's ages when the observations were made (Adam: 10¼, 12½, 14, 15, 17, 18½, 19, 21 months; William: 10½, 12½, 14, 15, 16½, 18, 19, 21 months). The sessions lasted for approximately 15 minutes and were recorded using a Sony Rover Kit 320 and a Sony solid state video-recorder 362 OCE.

Recordings were made of two situations. In one, the mother was asked to play with her child, in the other she was asked to read a picture-book. The mothers were left free to organize these situations in the way which best suited them and to use either their own toys or a selection provided by the observer.

Definitions of categories

The basic unit of behaviour used in the analysis was the *turn*. A *turn* was defined as a coherent unit of behaviour which could consist of either an act, a gesture or a vocalization occurring alone; an act accompanied by a vocalization; an act immediately followed by a related gesture and/or vocalization; or a co-occurring gesture and vocalization.

Acts and gestures

Acts and gestures were distinguished by their intention and point of focus. *Acts* achieved ends in themselves which were not primarily communicative, for instance, reaching for and grasping a toy. *Gestures* were used to signal intended meaning to another person, for example, opening and shutting the fist with the arm extended in the direction of a toy, while gaze alternated between the mother and the toy.

Taxonomy of gesture

Gestures were identified from their forms, the context in which they occurred and the effect they had on the mother. They were divided into four types.

Instrumental.   These are gestures which serve to change the behaviour of the partner. For example, the child raises his arms to his mother indicating a wish to be picked up, or the child uses a palm-away gesture to refuse the offer of a toy.

Expressive.   These are gestures which display the child's positive or negative feelings. For example, the child makes eye-contact and smiles broadly in an intentionally communicative manner to signal pleasure, or the child's face puckers and he stamps his feet angrily to convey displeasure.

Enactive.   These are gestures representing actions of people or actions on objects performed in imaginary contexts: for example, pretending to drink out of an empty cup, or pretending to walk a teddy bear round the palm of one's hand.

Deictic.   These gestures isolate an object from its general context. For example, the child points to an object, or shows an object in an extended hand. Particular attention was given to pointing gestures.

Vocalizations

In order to explore the relationship between gesture and vocalization, four stages of verbal development were identified.

Babbling.   Random vocalizations or strings of jargon with no sound–meaning regularity: for example, /ʌ/ used to accompany a variety of solitary or socially directed actions.

Proto-words.   Isolable utterances with relatively stable phonetic structure but unrelated to a target utterance in the adult language. Each proto-word occurs regularly in specific contexts, and each expresses a single communicative goal. For example, the sound /ɛ:/ or the more intense variant /ɛ:ɛ:/ to express that an object or service is wanted.

Conventional single-word utterances.   Imitations of adult words with allowances made for infant articulation and for overgeneralized or restricted use. Examples include the names of domestic objects, animals and action-type words such as 'no', 'more', 'up', and so forth.

Multi-word utterances.   Two or more words expressed within a single intonation pattern, for example, 'bubbles gone', 'more juice', 'Mummy do it'.

Unclear utterances.   Vocalizations occurring after the onset of conventional word usage that were poorly articulated and could be understood by neither the mother nor the observer.

Analyses

In the play situation, 100 'child turns' were transcribed from each session for analysis. Fewer interactions were generated in the book-reading situations which resulted in approximately 50 turns for each child. The corresponding 150 'mother turns' were transcribed in order to provide the context in which the child's signalling could be understood. The average inter-observer agreement for categorizing vocalizations, acts and gestures was 92 per cent. For the four gesture categories, the inter-observer agreement was: instrumental, 90 per cent; expressive, 85 per cent; enactive, 92 per cent; and deictic 93 per cent.

To test for differences between the children and the two contexts (play and picture-book), a two-way analysis of variance was conducted using the MINITAB package.

Results

General trends in the use of acts, gestures and vocalization are examined first, before considering each category of gesture in more detail.

Gesture in relation to acts and vocalizations

There were changes over time in the occurrence of acts, gestures and vocalizations. Acts predominated in the early sessions as can be seen in Fig. 1 but these declined, particularly in the picture-book situation. This reflects changes in the children's tendencies to use the book as a toy by opening and shutting it, or turning the pages indiscriminately. Gestures, which occurred relatively infrequently at first, increased between 10 and 18 months but then began to decline. Vocalizations showed a steady increase and by 21 months at least 70 per cent of the turns in the play situation, and 90 per cent in the picture-book situation, contained vocalizations. These occurred either alone or combined with gestures and the rate of vocalization was particularly high in the later sessions when gesture was declining. Gesture, particularly in the picture-book situation, became increasingly integrated with vocalization (Fig. 1).

The vocalizations accompanying gestures showed developmental changes over the 10–21-month period (Table 1). Proto-words were used by both children from the first play situation recorded. William was also producing some conventional utterances and babbling. The use of proto-words accompanying gestures in both contexts increased significantly with age for both children (William: $F = 3.84$, d.f. $= 7,7$, $P < 0.05$; Adam: $F = 5.91$, d.f. $= 7,7$, $P < 0.05$). Adam combined proto-words with gestures more than William did ($F = 13.58$, d.f. $= 1,7$, $P < 0.01$) in the play situation.

Proto-words continued to be used until about 19 months but they were gradually superseded by single-word utterances. The use of conventional words, as would be expected, increased with age, William ($F = 5.55$, d.f. $= 7,7$, $P < 0.05$) using them with gestures more often than Adam ($F = 7.22$, d.f. $= 1,7$, $P < 0.05$). Both children combined gestures and conventional words more frequently when reading picture-books than when playing (William: $F = 11.08$, d.f. $= 1,7$, $P < 0.05$; Adam: $F = 10.16$, d.f. $= 1,7$, $P < 0.05$). Multi-word utterances occurred in William's recording sessions from 18 months onwards, and in Adam's from 19 months.

Different types of gesture: Use and change over time

Gestural types varied in the time of their emergence, in the extent of their occurrence and

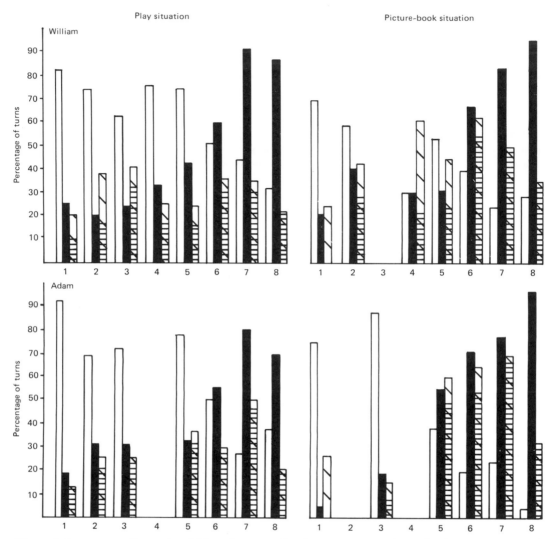

Figure 1. Percentage of turns in which actions, vocalizations, gestures and vocalized gestures occurred over the eight recording sessions. □, actions; ■, vocalizations; ◩, gestures; ▨, vocalized gestures.

the contexts in which they were used. Differences were also observed as to when and how often they were accompanied by vocalizations.

Instrumental gestures.   Instrumental gestures were used more frequently in the play than in the picture-book context (William: $F = 9.82$, d.f. = 1,7, $P < 0.05$; Adam: $F = 46.96$, d.f. = 1,7, $P < 0.01$). In the play situation, instrumental gestures increased significantly with age ($F = 17.05$, d.f. = 7,7, $P < 0.01$). From the first recording session, these gestures could be combined with vocalizations (Table 2).

Differences were apparent in the children's progression from proto-words to multi-word utterances accompanying instrumental gestures (Table 3). Adam largely used proto-words in conjunction with these gestures until, at 21 months, he used single and multi-word accompaniments. William combined some gestures with babbling and unclear vocalizations from 10 to 18 months, with the gesture not the vocalization carrying the meaning. He began using single-word conventional utterances at $12\frac{1}{2}$ months and multi-word utterances at 19 months. As with Adam, proto-words were evident until the final session at 21 months.

Table 1. Percentage of turns involving the use of gesture and different types of vocalization

	Play								Picture-book							
	1	2	3	4	5	6	7	8	1	2	3	4	5	6	7	8
William																
Proto-words	3	5	8	13	5	12	4	3	0	6	—	6	3	24	2	0
Conventional	2	8	12	2	6	12	19	8	0	20	—	4	16	22	30	20
Multi-word	0	0	0	0	0	0	9	6	0	0	—	0	0	4	10	10
Unclear/babbling	3	1	13	0	1	5	0	2	0	0	—	8	3	6	6	0
Total	8	14	33	15	12	29	32	19	0	26	—	18	22	56	48	30
Adam																
Proto-words	8	19	20	—	22	19	27	0	0	—	5	—	12	18	16	0
Conventional	0	1	4	—	6	6	13	5	0	—	4	—	31	32	42	24
Multi-word	0	0	0	—	0	0	0	11	0	—	0	—	0	0	3	8
Unclear/babbling	0	0	0	—	0	0	5	0	0	—	0	—	0	0	3	0
Total	8	20	24	—	28	25	45	16	0	—	9	—	43	50	64	32

Table 2. Frequency of turns in which gestural types occurred and the percentage accompanied by vocalizations

	Play								Picture-book							
	1	2	3	4	5	6	7	8	1	2	3	4	5	6	7	8
William																
Instrumental	3	20	5	5	4	10	14	2	0	4	—	2	1	0	1	1
% vocalized	100	65	80	100	75	70	100	100	0	50	—	50	100	0	100	100
Expressive	4	10	11	3	5	12	4	3	0	4	—	1	1	3	0	1
% vocalized	75	10	91	33	80	92	100	100	0	75	—	0	100	66	0	100
Enactive	9	5	6	5	9	2	7	6	0	0	—	5	1	5	2	0
% vocalized	20	0	50	20	22	100	85	10	0	0	—	66	100	80	100	0
Deictic	2	3	18	11	4	10	9	10	4	13	—	23	15	22	21	14
% vocalized	0	0	87	73	75	90	80	80	0	60	—	27	60	95	93	100
No. of turns	100	100	100	100	100	100	100	100	17	50	—	50	38	50	50	50
Adam																
Instrumental	10	26	14	—	25	13	20	6	0		0	—	2	3	0	0
% vocalized	70	77	86	—	80	92	95	100	0	—	0	—	100	100	0	0
Expressive	2	0	2	—	2	1	1	1	0	—	1	—	0	1	0	0
% vocalized	50	0	100	—	100	0	0	0	0	—	0	—	0	100	0	0
Enactive	0	0	0	—	0	3	0	0	0	—	0	—	0	0	0	0
% vocalized	0	0	0	—	0	100	0	0	0	—	0	—	0	0	0	0
Deictic	0	0	10	—	8	20	28	10	5	—	6	—	19	28	22	16
% vocalized	0	0	100	—	75	100	93	100	0	—	80	—	80	82	94	100
No. of turns	100	100	100	—	100	100	100	100	20	—	50	—	36	50	33	55

Throughout the observation sessions, the vocal and gestural mode generally conveyed the same meaning. For example, Adam always accompanied his reaching/opening/shutting fist gesture with the proto-word /əhɛ/. In the last session, however, the verbal and gestural forms were also used to complement the meanings each expressed thus conveying a more complex idea than would have been achieved by each singly. This can be seen in the following exchange between William and his mother:

Mother: William:
Billy choose one

No   (shakes his head)
Book (takes his mother's hand and places it on the pile)

Table 3. Types of vocalization occurring in conjunction with gestures in the play situation (percentages)

	William								Adam							
	1	2	3	4	5	6	7	8	1	2	3	4	5	6	7	8
Instrumental																
Proto-words	66	31	25	80	33	86	14	0	100	95	100	—	100	100	100	0
Conventional	0	62	25	20	66	0	50	0	0	5	0	—	0	0	0	17
Multi-word	0	0	0	0	0	0	36	100	0	0	0	—	0	0	0	83
Unclear/babbling	33	7	50	0	0	14	0	0	0	0	0	—	0	0	0	0
Expressive																
Proto-words	33	100	50	100	75	27	0	66	100	0	100	—	100	0	0	0
Conventional	0	0	10	0	0	64	100	33	0	0	0	—	0	0	0	0
Multi-word	0	0	0	0	0	0	0	0	0	0	0	—	0	0	0	0
Unclear/babbling	66	0	40	0	25	9	0	0	0	0	0	—	0	0	0	0
Enactive																
Proto-words	0	0	0	100	50	0	0	0	0	0	0	—	0	0	0	0
Conventional	100	0	100	0	50	50	66	66	0	0	0	—	0	100	0	0
Multi-word	0	0	0	0	0	0	33	33	0	0	0	—	0	0	0	0
Unclear/babbling	0	0	0	0	0	50	0	0	0	0	0	—	0	0	0	0
Deictic																
Proto-words	0	0	14	87	0	33	25	12	0	0	60	—	0	70	31	0
Conventional	0	0	36	13	100	44	50	38	0	0	40	—	100	30	50	40
Multi-word	0	0	0	0	0	0	25	25	0	0	0	—	0	0	0	60
Unclear/babbling	0	0	50	0	0	22	0	25	0	0	0	—	0	0	29	0

The utterance 'book' gives the name of the object being negotiated. The gesture indicates who shall perform the action (the mother) and what action is required (picking up the book). Together, action and gesture convey the message 'You choose the book Mummy'.

Expressive gestures. William used expressive gestures more than Adam (play: $F= 12\cdot37$, d.f. $= 1,7$, $P < 0\cdot05$; picture-book: $F= 7\cdot00$, d.f. $= 1,7$, $P < 0\cdot05$) and both children used them more frequently when playing (William: $F= 25\cdot93$, d.f. $= 1,7$, $P < 0\cdot01$; Adam: $F= 6\cdot24$, d.f. $= 1,7$, $P < 0\cdot05$).

From 10 months, both children were able to coordinate expressive gestures with vocalizations (Table 2). Initially proto-words occurred in conjunction with William's expressive gestures, though conventional words occurred with them from 18 months (Table 3). When proto-words accompanied expressive gestures both conveyed the same meaning. For example, William would wave his arms up and down while repeating /hɔhɔhɔhɔ/ with increasing intensity to express pleasure. Conventional words used with expressive gestures could convey the same feelings as the gesture, or function as labels, as in the following example:

Mother:	William:
(Offers William a bag of toys)	Ooh (flutters arms excitedly)
	(takes out bottle of bubbles and hands it to his mother)
Ooh, what is it?	
Bubbles	/bʌbə/ (bubbles) (flutters his arms excitedly)

Enactive gestures. Adam used enactive gestures in just one session, when he was $18\frac{1}{2}$ months (Table 2). William used enactive gestures from $10\frac{1}{2}$ months in the play situation and from 15 months in the book situation. Their use fluctuated from session to session but they occurred more frequently in the play context ($F= 9\cdot07$, d.f. $= 1,7$, $P < 0\cdot05$).

William could combine enactive gestures with vocalizations at $10\frac{1}{2}$ months but only did so with less than 50 per cent of gestures until 18 months when coordination fluctuated between 85 and 100 per cent (Table 2). Conventional single-word utterances co-occurred with enactive gestures at $10\frac{1}{2}$ months, and multi-words at 19 months (Table 3). Proto-words were used only twice.

Initially, both vocalization and gesture conveyed the same meaning. For example, William at 15 months would hug his doll and say 'Ah'; Adam at 18 months pushed his fire-engine saying 'Bi-bi, bi-bi'. At 21 months William used words and gestures with each contributing a particular aspect to the total meaning. For instance, while pretending to pour from a coffee pot and stirring in an empty cup, he said, 'Cook ... there ... more'. To express the idea that his ball had got dirty when he dropped it in the mud, he dropped the piece of plasticene he had been playing with and said, 'Go, yugh'.

Deictic gestures. These showed a significant increase over time (William: $F = 4\cdot26$, d.f. $= 7,7$, $P < 0\cdot05$; Adam: $F = 5\cdot46$, d.f. $= 7,7$, $P < 0\cdot05$). Both children could use deictic gestures at 10 months although Adam did not use them in the play situation until he was 14 months (Table 2). In the play situation, showing and pointing were used initially only to indicate objects of mutual interest. Half way through the sessions, points were also used to indicate objects that the child wanted, generally in alternation with reaching gestures if the sequence lasted for some time. There was no significant difference in the extent to which both children used deictic gestures but with William they occurred more frequently when he was looking at books ($F = 19\cdot63$, d.f. $= 1,7$, $P < 0\cdot01$).

Although William's early deictic gestures were not observed in conjunction with vocalizations, from 14 months onwards a very high proportion of deictic gestures and vocalizations occurred together in both William's and Adam's exchanges with their mothers (Table 2). Proto-words and conventional words were coordinated with deictic gestures from 14 months, multi-words emerging towards the end of the recording sessions (Table 3).

As with the other types of gesture, deictic gesture and vocalization, initially used separately, became coordinated to convey the same or complementary meanings. Deictic gestures first served to indicate objects of interest. This function continued when the gestures were combined with a vocalization, both expressing the same meaning whether a proto-word or conventional word was used. For example, Adam accompanied early points with /ɔ/ or /æt/, the latter form, being an approximation of 'that', gaining in precedence. Similarly, when pointing or showing was used in a labelling or heuristic context, the point or showing gesture isolated the referent, and the utterance added the function of naming or requesting a name.

When request for an object was signalled, gestural points and vocalizations contributed complementary meanings. Pointing identified the location and the vocalization expressed the request. Adam, for instance, initially accompanied location pointing with the vocalization which typically went with reaching gestures, /ɔhɛː/; later, points were accompanied by the name of the requested object.

Examining pointing more specifically (Table 4), the same general developmental trend is reflected: pointing gestures declined as the rate of vocalization increased and vocabulary acquisition accelerated. The picture-book situation, however, showed a significant increase in pointing over time ($F = 4\cdot84$; d.f. $= 7,7$, $P < 0\cdot05$). There was no difference between the children in the extent to which they used pointing gestures and, as would be expected, they occurred more frequently in the picture-book context (William: $F = 48\cdot05$, d.f. $= 1,7$, $P < 0\cdot01$; Adam: $F = 10\cdot63$, d.f. $= 1,7$, $P < 0\cdot05$).

Proximal pointing emerged before distal pointing (Table 4). William used proximal points at $10\frac{1}{2}$ months and distal points in the third recording session when he was 14 months. Although Adam did not use any index finger points in the first book-reading

Table 4. Percentage of turns containing points

Session	Play situation					Picture-book situation				
	Total	Alone	+ Voc.	Proximal	Distal	Total	Alone	+ Voc.	Proximal	Distal
William										
1	2	2	0	2	0	15	15	0	15	0
2	0	0	0	0	0	14	6	8	14	0
3	4	0	4	1	3	—	—	—	—	—
4	5	1	4	3	2	44	32	12	40	4
5	0	0	0	0	0	35	15	20	32	3
6	9	0	9	7	2	44	2	42	40	4
7	3	0	3	3	0	42	3	39	42	0
8	10	0	10	6	4	28	0	28	28	0
Total	33	3	30	22	11	222	73	149	211	11
Adam										
1	0	0	0	0	0	0	0	0	0	0
2	0	0	0	0	0	—	—	—	—	—
3	10	1	9	8	2	10	2	8	10	0
4	—	—	—	—	—	—	—	—	—	—
5	1	0	1	1	0	50	10	40	46	4
6	10	0	10	9	1	56	10	46	50	6
7	28	1	27	8	20	66	4	62	58	8
8	10	0	10	8	2	32	0	32	28	4
Total	59	2	57	34	25	214	26	188	192	22

session, 10 per cent of the turns had full hand-patting gestures functioning to indicate referents that his mother had just isolated. Unfortunately, there are no data available for session 2, but by 14 months, in the third session, Adam was using both proximal and distal points. Proximal points occurred more frequently in the picture-book context (William: $F = 58·66$, d.f. $= 1,7$, $P < 0·01$; Adam: $F = 6·56$, d.f. $= 1,7$, $P < 0·05$). Proximal pointing increased over time in both children (play: $F = 5·65$, d.f. $= 7,7$, $P < 0·05$; picture-book: $F = 3·79$, d.f. $= 7,7$, $P < 0·05$).

When reading books, proximal points were generally responses to the mother's request to indicate a named object, or were used when the child wanted to comment on or ask about a picture. Distal points indicated real objects, depicted in the book, which were located in the house or garden.

In the play situation between 90 and 100 per cent of pointing gestures were accompanied by vocalizations. In the early picture-book sessions, coordinated use of points and vocalizations was less than this, probably because of the nature of the situation. For instance, when pointing occurred alone it was usually a response to the mother's request to locate a feature she had named. Pointing accompanied by vocalization showed a significant increase with age for both children ($F = 12·98$, d.f. $= 7,7$, $P < 0·01$), there being no difference between the children in the extent to which they combined the two expressions. However, when the kinds of words accompanying pointing were examined, it was found that Adam, with his later acquisition of conventional words, was accompanying his points only with variations of /æt/—/ǽt/ signalling 'look at that', and /ǽt/ signalling 'what is that?'. William, by contrast, was accompanying his points with a wide variety of labelling terms referring to animals, people and domestic items.

Discussion and conclusions

Our observations indicate the increasing coordination of verbal and non-verbal modes and the elaboration that marked the communicative exchanges between the infants and their mothers. The decline of acts, initially a basis on which mothers impute meaning, can be viewed in relation to the increase of gestures, particularly in the picture-book situation. Similarly, the dramatic rise in vocalizations over the 10–21-month period, their increasing coordination with gestures and the signs of a decline in gestures at 21 months suggest a gradual and subtle progress from non-verbal to verbal communication.

Proto-words were the predominant form of vocalization occurring at the time when gestures were used most frequently. During this period the gesture was generally the easier to understand of the two modes—the gestures being potent signals in themselves, with or without a vocalization. This is partly because of the lack of clear differentiation between proto-words, and partly because the child's needs are linked to and fairly easily interpretable within well-established contexts.

Furthermore, proto-words are limited in their function (Dore *et al.*, 1976). When conventional utterances emerge, these too are limited initially in their communicative range (Halliday, 1975; Lock, 1978, 1980). For several months, for instance, object words may be used only to label and not to request. Until words become plurifunctional—that is, they can be used to express a variety of functions—gestures continue to have an important complementary role in all the four gestural categories we have discussed.

Gestures declined when Adam and William began to use words in a plurifunctional manner and when their rate of vocalization and vocabulary size had markedly increased At 10 months, William had three conventional single words, Adam none. By 21 months, estimates based on mothers' records and recorded observations showed William to have a vocabulary size of about 190 words, while Adam was approaching 250.

Changes were evident in the relationship between the two modes which reflected increasing complexity over time. Initially the gesture and vocalization, whether proto-word or conventional word, conveyed the same meaning. From the middle of the second year, once the two modes were integrated, word and gesture began to convey separate aspects of a message. Carter (1978) found with the infant she studied that there was tight bonding between gestural and verbal forms up to the age of 16 months. This tight bonding seems to break down as words and gestures each come to be used for a variety of functions and can enter into more flexible relationships with other communication forms.

The integration of verbal and gestural modes, evident in all four types of gesture, showed certain differences in the times when coordination was established. By 10 months, instrumental and expressive gestures were being used with vocalizations. As verbal capacity increased, words could be used to express requests, needs and interests more specifically and economically than gestures alone could convey messages. Whilst the use of early forms diminishes, other forms of instrumental and expressive gestures may develop later. These more conventionalized forms may be used to emphasize verbal messages or even be used instead of words. Michael & Willis (1968), for example, describe 12 common gestures used by 4–7-year-old children to signal 'Be quiet', 'Go away', 'Come here', etc. Expressive gestures, unintentionally emitted as expressions of anxiety, or conventionalized forms such as the clenched fist, are observable in adults (Barten, 1977).

Enactive gestures appeared to depend on encouragement more than the others. Adam could use them, but hardly ever did because his mother did not provide the same eliciting conditions as William's mother. Enactive and deictic gestures, whose emergence and coordination with vocalization occurred slightly later than instrumental and expressive gestures, continued to be used even when words became the dominant form of expression. In addition to their initial use in imaginative play, enactive gestures were used for explicitly communicative functions by William. He requested objects and actions, and expressed the activities of picture-book characters by using enactive gestures. Enactive gestures continue in the context of pretend play, developing in complexity and range (McCune-Nicolich, 1981).

Contrary to Barten's (1977) assumptions, we did not find that deictic gestures were the first to emerge. Like Masur (1983) we found that instrumental gestures, such as offering objects and reaching, were functioning before pointing and showing gestures. Similarly, expressive gestures, and in William's case, enactive gestures, appeared at 10 months whereas pointing initiated by the child was not firmly established until 14 months. Pointing was predictive of the onset of language, reflecting the suggestions made by Bates *et al.* (1979). William started to use index finger pointing gestures before Adam, and acquired his first words and reached the 50-word level before Adam. However, although at 18 months there were great differences in their vocabulary size (William, approximately 77 words; Adam, approximately 22 words) by 21 months Adam had far surpassed William (William, 190 words; Adam, 250).

When pointing first emerged as an intentionally signalled behaviour, it was not used with vocalizations in either the play situation or in the picture-book situation, but rather as an imitation of the mother's deictic gestures. At about 14 months, when used in conjunction with vocalizations, pointing continued to convey the single function of indicating. Proximal and distal points covering varying distances and orientations were both understood and produced, supporting the findings of Murphy & Messer (1977) and Lempers (1979). Also, dual directional signalling, involving eye-gaze and pointing in different directions, had emerged (Masur, 1983). Coordination of conventional words with gestures was established within about three weeks and points then began to serve a number of functions: to label, to ask for information and to request. Points were used with a wide variety of words with the two modes conveying either the same or complementary meanings. Deictic gestures continued well into the multi-word period, continuing to be used to convey deictic contrasts which are beyond the linguistic capacity of the child (Bloom, 1970; E. V. Clark & Sengul, 1978).

Gesture plays an important role in enhancing the effectiveness of communication in the proto-language period. Initially, it may be used on its own, or is easier to understand than the vocal signal it accompanies. Later it serves to reinforce the verbal message or to add to the notion being signalled verbally. But gestures, or at least the four kinds witnessed during the proto-language period, are limited in their referential capacity. For words to function as autonomous symbols, Dore *et al.* (1976) suggest that expressions must indicate and provide some differentiation among alternatives. Instrumental and expressive gestures, although successful in communicating general meanings of likes and dislikes, of wanting and rejection, do not fulfil either criterion. Deictic gestures certainly indicate, but without accompanying words cannot automatically be assumed to be differentiating among alternatives. It is only enactive gestures that convey such specificity of meaning; but they too are limited in that they convey only the *actions* of objects and people, and not the *characteristics* of the objects themselves. Depictive gestures which could function as fully 'linguistic' symbols have not yet emerged by 21 months when the hearing child begins to use multi-word expressions (Franklin, 1973).

Although gestures appear to have antecedents in earlier non-functional movements or technical actions, some seem to rely more on modelling by the caregiver for their emergence. Whilst instrumental and expressive gestures may well be shaped by the responsiveness of the mother in regarding them as signals, mothers do not appear to be providing direct models for these gestures. Mothers are never observed to clench and unclench their fists when requesting, or to flap their arms to indicate pleasure. By contrast, deictic and enactive gestures are modelled and specifically encouraged by the mothers.

Although the mother's responses may be significant in shaping gestural usage, individual differences are also apparent. This study has highlighted temperamental differences that may account for the range and extent to which expressive and instrumental gestures are used. But differences may also be related to the rate at which verbal development occurs. Adam, although initially slower at acquiring words, soon caught up with and outstripped William, and the decline in gesture occurred at similar ages for both children. However, one could envisage that, where vocabulary acquisition is more gradual, the use of gesture would be prolonged and a richer repertoire might be developed to compensate for deficiencies in the linguistic mode.

Language does not arise in a vacuum. The development of gesture shows the emergence of a form of communication that can indeed lead to language without speech (Bellugi & Klima, 1984). Gestural development shows similarities with the acquisition of language in that single expressions are followed by the coordinated use of increasingly conventionalized forms to convey an increasingly complex range of meaning (Martlew, in press). Non-conventional forms, such as proto-words, instrumental reaching or arm flapping, disappear after serving temporary and limited functions. Some gestures die out because the contexts in which they were used tend to disappear—such as many of the contrived game situations appropriate only to infancy. The child progresses to a level at which he or she is ready to embark on using symbols in a linguistic manner.

Whilst individual means to achieve communicative ends may vary, they serve the purpose of extending communicative flexibility and shared meaning. In this study, for instance, expressive and enactive gestures were not important means for Adam, whereas William practised and elaborated these gestures. However, it is also appreciated that deictic gestures, which designate specific focused reference, encouraged the use of conventional vocabulary and provided a facilitating framework for substitution. The transition from pointing alone to pointing in combination with conventional words is possibly the gateway to the ultimate goal of linguistic communication.

This goal, however, is too important to be left totally to chance environmental fluctuations and there are many routes for the child's developing awareness of communicative strategies. When children start to acquire language they have already experienced many ways of effecting communicative exchanges. In beginning the search for linguistic data to serve communicative ends, they have a range of experiences to help them know which they are looking for. Children's entry into the linguistic system comes at a time when they can capitalize on the established framework of integrated and increasingly conventionalized signals while drawing on higher order cognitive skills and emerging linguistic processing capacity.

Acknowledgement

This work was assisted in part by a grant from the Spastics Society.

References

Barten, S. (1977). The development of gesture. In N. R. Smith & M. B. Franklin (eds), *Symbolic Functioning in Childhood*. Hillsdale, NJ: Erlbaum.

Bates, E., Benigni, L., Bretherton, I., Camaioni, L. & Volterra, V. (1977). From gesture to first word: On cognitive and social prerequisites. In M. Lewis & L. Rosenblum (eds), *Interaction, Conversation and the Development of Language*. New York: Wiley.

Bates, E., Benigni, L., Bretherton, I., Camaioni, L. & Volterra, V. (1979). *The Emergence of Symbols: Communication and Cognition in Infancy*. New York: Academic Press.

Bates, E., Bretherton, I., Snyder, L., Shore, C. & Volterra, V. (1980). Vocal and gestural symbols at 13 months. *Merrill–Palmer Quarterly*, **26**, 407–423.

Bates, E., Camaioni, I. & Volterra, V. (1975). The acquisition of performatives prior to speech. *Merrill–Palmer Quarterly*, **21**, 206–226.

Bellugi, U. & Klima, E.S. (1984). Signed and spoken language: Comparison of developmental processes. Paper presented at the meeting on Language Development and Communication Problems of the Handicapped, Oxford.

Bloom, L. M. (1970). *Language Development: Form and Function in Emerging Grammars*. Cambridge, MA: MIT.

Bruner, J. (1975). The ontogenesis of speech acts. *Journal of Child Language*, **2**, 1–19.

Carter, A. L. (1978). From sensorimotor morphemes to words. In A. L. Lock (ed.), *Action, Gesture and Symbol: The Emergence of Language*. London: Academic Press.

Clark, E.V. & Sengul, C. J. (1978). Strategies in the acquisition of deixis. *Journal of Child Language*, **5**, 457–475.

Clark, R. A. (1978). The transition from action to gesture. In A. Lock (ed.), *Action, Gesture and Symbol: The Emergence of Language*. London: Academic Press.

Escalona, S. (1973). Basic modes of social interaction: Their emergence and patterning during the first two years of life. *Merrill–Palmer Quarterly*, **19**, 205–232.

Dore, J., Franklin, M., Miller, R. & Ramer, A. L. M. (1976). Transitional phenomena in early language acquisition. *Journal of Child Language*, **3**, 13–28.

Ferguson, C. A. (1976). Learning to pronounce: The earliest stages of phonological development in the child. *Stanford Papers and Reports on Child Language Development*, 11.

Fogel, A. (1981). The ontogeny of gestural communication: The first six months. In R. Stark (ed.), *Language Behavior in Infancy and Early Childhood*. New York: Elsevier.

Franklin, M. B. (1973). Non-verbal representation in young children: A cognitive perspective. *Young Children*, **11**, 33–53.

Halliday, M. (1975). *Learning How to Mean: Explorations in the Development of Language*. London: Arnold.

Kaye, K. (1982). *The Mental and Social Life of Babies*. London: Methuen.

Lempers, J. D. (1979). Young children's production and comprehension of non-verbal (deictic) behaviours. *Journal of Genetic Psychology*, **135**, 93–102.

Leung, E. H. L. & Rheingold, H. L. (1981). The development of pointing as a social gesture. *Developmental Psychology*, **17**, 215–220.

Lock, A. (1978) (ed.) *Action, Gesture and Symbol: The Emergence of Language*. London: Academic Press.

Lock, A. (1980). *The Guided Reinvention of Language*. London: Academic Press.

Lockman, J. L. & Ashmead, D. H. (1983). Asynchronies in the development of manual behavior. In L. Lipsitt & C. K. Rovee-Collier (eds), *Advances in Infancy Research*, vol. 2. Norwood, NJ: Ablex.

Martlew, M. (in press). Prelinguistic communication. In M. Rutter, B. Yule & M. Bax (eds), *Language Development and Disorders*. London: Blackwell/SIMP.

McCune-Nicolich, L. (1981). Towards symbolic functioning: Structure of early pretend games and potential parallels with language. *Child Development*, **52**(3), 785–798.

Masur, E. F. (1982). Mothers' responses to infants' object-related gestures: Influences on lexical development. *Journal of Child Language*, **9**, 23–30.

Masur, E. F. (1983). Gestural development, dual-directional signalling, and the transition to words. *Journal of Psycholinguistic Research*, **12**(2), 93–109.

Michael, G. & Willis, F. (1968). Development of gestures as a function of social class, education, and sex. *Psychological Record*, **18**, 515-519.

Murphy, C. M. (1978). Pointing in the context of a shared activity. *Child Development*, **49**, 371–380.

Murphy, C. M. & Messer, D. J. (1977). Mothers, infants and pointing: A study of gesture. In H. R. Schaffer (ed.), *Studies in Mother–Infant Interaction*. London: Academic Press.

Stark, R. (1979). Prespeech segmental feature production. In P. Fletcher & M. Garman (eds), *Language Acquisition*. Cambridge: Cambridge University Press.

Thelen, E. (1981). Rhythmical behaviour in infancy: An ethological perspective. *Developmental Psychology*, **17**(3), 237–257.

Trevarthen, C. (1979). Communication and co-operation in early infancy: A description of primary intersubjectivity. In M. Bullowa (ed.), *Before Speech: The Beginnings of Interpersonal Communication*. Cambridge: Cambridge University Press.

Zinober, B. & Martlew, M. (1985). The development of communicative gestures. In M. Barrett (ed.), *Children's Single Word Speech*. Chichester: Wiley.

Requests for reprints should be addressed to Margaret Martlew, Department of Psychology, University of Sheffield, Sheffield S10 2TN, UK.

Brenda Zinober is also at the above address.

British Journal of Developmental Psychology (1985), **3**, 307–316   *Printed in Great Britain*

Emotional behaviour during the learning of a contingency in early infancy

Michael Lewis, Margaret Wolan Sullivan and **Jeanne Brooks-Gunn**

Sixty infants divided equally among three age groups (10, 16 and 24 weeks) participated in a contingency learning task. After an initial baseline period, half of the subjects received an audio-visual stimulus contingent upon arm movement while the remaining infants, matched for age and sex, served as a control group. Session length was controlled by the infant and served as an index of task involvement. Amount of visual fixation per minute, fussing and frequency of smiling were also examined. There were consistent condition effects for each of the arm movement measures analysed but age and age × condition effects were obtained only for average rate and peak rate of response. With respect to affective measures, subjects in the contingent condition spent more time in the experiment irrespective of age and fussed proportionally less compared with control subjects. These subjects at 16 and 24 weeks also smiled more than non-contingent controls at the same ages, although the overall rate of smiling was low.

Lewis (Lewis & Goldberg, 1969; Lewis, 1978; Lewis & Coates, 1980) and Watson (1972, 1977) have proposed that a contingently responsive environment results not only in cognitive consequences but also in motivational change. Specifically, a contingently responsive environment establishes an expectation of control over the environment—the opposite of learned helplessness (Seligman, 1975). Furthermore, Lewis & Goldberg (1969) proposed that this generalized expectation or feeling of efficacy should be accompanied by increased positive affect and enhanced task involvement. Task involvement was defined either as increased task attention or as more rapid habituation to redundant stimuli.

Increased positive affect directly associated with contingent stimulation was reported by Uzgiris & Hunt (1970) and by Watson (1972). In the course of two weeks of experience with a rotating mobile, an increased incidence of smiling and cooing was reported by Watson only among those infants who experienced activation of the mobile contingent on pillow presses. Like Lewis & Goldberg (1969), Watson (1977) argued that contingent environments lead to displays of positive affect. Sullivan *et al.* (1979) experimentally confirmed that smiling and vocalizing of 12-week-old infants increased over daily conditioning sessions. Brinker & Lewis (1982a) have also reported increased smiling and vocalizing and decreased crying when young, severely handicapped infants and toddlers experienced simple contingencies in a long-term contingency intervention programme.

While the evidence indicates that positive emotion accompanies contingency learning, two aspects of this relationship have not been systematically explored in early infancy: first, the consequences of contingent learning on the various emotional behaviours of the infant and, second, variations in emotional responses expressed during such learning as a function of age. Such affective consequences of contingency experience are of interest both in the light of the relationship between emotion and cognition that has been proposed by numerous developmental theorists (Kagan, 1974; Zajonc, 1980; Lazarus, 1982; Lewis & Michalson, 1983), and of the proposed link between early contingency experience and the subsequent motivational disposition of the infant (R. White, 1959; Lewis & Goldberg, 1969). This study examines task involvement, and affective and attentional responses that accompany a simple contingency experience at 10, 16 and 24 weeks of age. We hypothesized that exposure to contingent stimulation would be associated with increased time spent in the procedure, decreased fussiness and increased displays of positive affect (smiling) during the session.

Method

Subjects

Sixty infants—20 at each of three ages (10, 16 and 24 weeks)—were recruited via birth records published in local newspapers. The mean ages for subjects were 10·4 weeks (± 1 week), 15·9 weeks (± 1 week), and 23·6 weeks (± 1 week), respectively. All were full-term, Caucasian, middle-class, normal, healthy infants residing within travelling distance of the infant laboratory. Each age group consisted of equal numbers of male and female infants. A number of additional infants (28 per cent of the total subject pool) were tested at each age but were excluded from the final sample for fussiness either upon arrival at the laboratory or during baseline (eight infants at 10 weeks, one at 16 weeks and ten at 24 weeks), equipment problems (four infants) or drowsy inactivity (two infants). Subject loss occurred in the same proportion from both the contingent and non-contingent control groups.

Apparatus

The apparatus consisted of a three-sided enclosure housing an infant seat that faced a rear projection screen (18 cm square) mounted in the rear wall of the booth. The seat was 45 cm from the screen. A speaker (8 ohm) was mounted above the screen. A ribbon connected to a Velcro wrist-cuff worn on one arm by the subject emerged just below the screen and activated a microswitch mounted behind the booth wall. A pulling movement of the arm triggered a 3 s presentation of a colour slide of an infant's happy face, accompanied by a recording of children's voices singing the *Sesame Street* theme song. Following Millar (1972), sufficient ribbon slack was maintained so that hand to mouth activity would not produce a response. A small slot in the wall of the booth permitted unobtrusive observation of attentional and affective responses.

Measures

An arm-pull was chosen as the response since it is functional across a broad age span and can be conditioned in infants between 4 and 8 months (Millar, 1972). Arm-pulling is also a response with some ecological validity since it is during the period 8–16 weeks that infants typically begin to swipe at objects and when visually directed reaching is ultimately attained (B. L. White *et al.*, 1964). Arm-pull responses and length of session were automatically coded on-line. In addition, the frequency of smiling responses, frequency and duration of fussing and duration of attention to the contingency task were coded on-line by a trained observer who was naïve with regard to the hypotheses. The following definitions of behaviours were used:

Smiles/laughs was scored when the corners of the mouth were drawn up and outwards. The mouth could be either open or closed, but was typically open.

Fusses/frets was defined as a puckered face, involving wrinkling of the skin around the eyes, mouth and/or brows accompanied by repeated bursts of sounds, usually of similar pitch, with a general quality of dissatisfaction.

Attention was scored when the infant's head and eyes were orientated towards the feedback location (i.e. the speaker or the screen).

Reliability was calculated for the complete sessions of three randomly selected infants. The sessions at which a second observer was present totalled some 70 min of observation time. Proportion of inter-rater agreement was calculated for each measure (agreements/agreements + disagreements). Agreement on the frequency of smiling behaviour ranged from 0·80 to 0·83 with a mean of 0·81. Agreement on the frequency of fuss/cries exceeded 0·80 and averaged 0·81. This level of reliability is consistent with that previously reported for these measures (Rovee-Collier & Fagen, 1976; Sullivan, 1982). Since a low frequency of smiling or fussy behaviour may have resulted in spuriously high reliabilities if 'no response' was scored consistently, a *t* test was conducted to determine whether the actual frequency of either behaviour differed between observers. In fact, there was no difference. Reliability was also calculated for duration of attention and duration of fusses/cries. Agreement for duration of attention to task consistently exceeded 0·90 with a mean of 0·96, while the agreement for fusses/cries was 0·90.

Procedure

Subjects matched for age and sex were randomly assigned to either a contingent (experimental) or non-contingent (control) condition. Infants in both conditions were placed in the apparatus; however, only infants in the contingent group were capable of activating the audio-visual display. Infants in the non-contingent condition had no control over the stimuli. Instead, an audiotape of responses produced by their contingent partner was played back for the duration of the session. The tape also triggered slide onsets. Non-contingent subjects received rates of stimulation similar to that of the contingent subjects but, unlike the contingent group, their stimulation was independent of their response rate. A perfectly matched control or yoked group was not possible given our variable of time in the task. Imagine an experimental subject whose time in the study was only 5 min. If we provided the control with the exact same condition, it could by definition last only 5 min. In order to avoid the problem of truncating control subjects' sessions, only the stimulus tapes of experimental subjects who stayed in the study longer than 10 min were used. These tapes played back the exact rate and number for the control which was obtained by the experimental subject. This 10 min minimum was decided upon since 9–15 min of exposure to the contingent stimulus has been used previously both in our work and in the literature, and has been found to result in learning. In fact, only two contingent subjects each at 10 and 24 weeks of age and three at 16 weeks failed to attain this 10 min criterion. Thus, only 23 per cent of non-contingent subjects did not receive a perfect match but were randomly assigned another contingent tape of an infant of the same age and sex. By using a control tape of an infant who remained in the study longer than the 'true' match, it would appear that the procedure favoured the control subjects.

For all subjects, each session included a 60 s baseline period and an individually variable period of stimulation. Criteria for the termination of the procedure were 30 s of continuous fussy behaviour, 30 s of eyes closed, or 2·5 min of arm inactivity. For 95 per cent of all cases, however, the session was terminated for fussiness. The fact that subjects were permitted to remain in the apparatus for as long as they appeared interested and did not fuss is a departure from most studies of contingent learning which typically employ fixed session lengths. Variable session length in fact allows the child another dimension of control and provides an index of task persistence and/ or interest.

Results

Repeated measures analyses of variance were conducted for each dependent variable (i.e. time in experiment, the arm-pull measures, and measures of affect and attention) over factors of age (3), sex (2) and condition (2).

Task involvement: Time in experiment and subject drop-out

Fifty per cent of non-contingent controls dropped out of the experiment by the end of minute 10, whereas 50 per cent of the contingent subjects did not drop out until after minute 16. Contingent subjects averaged 14·4 minutes in the session, range 8–36 minutes; non-contingent controls averaged 8·4 minutes, range 4–19 minutes. Though the longest session occurred for a 24-week-old, three of the 10-week-old contingent subjects exceeded 25 minutes in the session.

Contingent subjects spent more time in the procedure than non-contingent controls ($F = 26·27$, d.f. = 1, 24, $P < 0·0001$). As shown in Fig. 1, at each age infants receiving contingent stimulation were those most willing to remain in the apparatus (10 weeks: $t = 3·34$, d.f. = 9, $P < 0·01$; 16 weeks: $t = 2·53$, d.f. = 9, $P < 0·01$; 24 weeks: $t = 2·82$, d.f. = 9, $P < 0·01$). A sex × condition interaction was also found ($F = 4·89$, d.f. = 1, 24, $P < 0·04$) such that male subjects remained in the procedure longer than female contingent subjects ($t = 1·98$, d.f. = 14, $P < 0·05$) but tended to terminate their sessions sooner than non-contingent females ($t = 1·45$, d.f. = 14, $P < 0·10$).

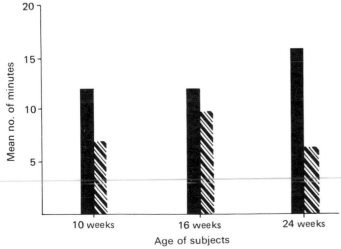

Figure 1. Mean time (minutes) spent in the experiment at 10, 16 and 24 weeks of age. ■, contingent; ◧, non-contingent.

Arm-pull analyses

Minute-by-minute analyses were first conducted over the first four minutes of the experiment (i.e. baseline and the first three minutes of the stimulus period) when a complete subject complement was available for both control and contingent subjects. (Non-contingent controls began to drop out from the fourth minute so that minute-by-minute analyses could not be conducted beyond this point.) There were no group differences during baseline or the initial minutes of the session except for the 24-week-old contingent subjects who showed a trend of increased arm-pulling over the first four minutes ($F = 3.00$, d.f. $= 2, 24$, $P < 0.08$). The lack of an increase over the first four minutes is not unusual, particularly for younger subjects, since Millar (1972) who examined arm-pull data by three-minute acquisition blocks observed a significant increase in only one out of three groups of 4-month-old subjects that received contingent stimulation.

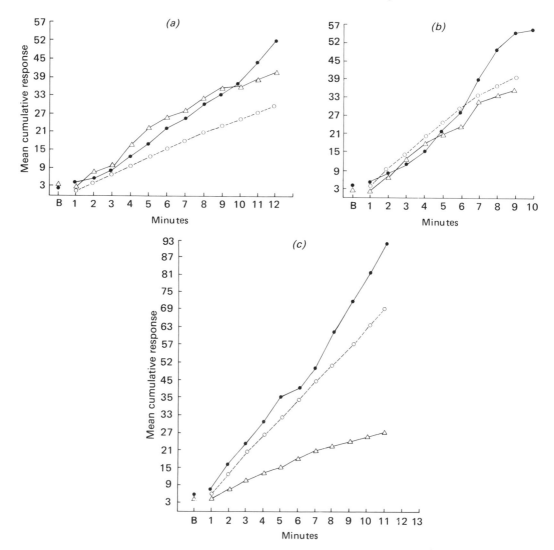

Figure 2. Cumulative response curves at (*a*) 10 weeks, (*b*) 16 weeks and (*c*) 24 weeks over time. Curves terminate at the point at which 30 per cent of contingent subjects in each group have fussed to criterion. Expected curves for contingent subjects are generated from baseline data. ●——●, contingent; △——△, non-contingent; ○----○, expected contingent.

Figure 2 presents the cumulative response curves of contingent and non-contingent subjects at each age. Also depicted is an 'expected' cumulative curve. The latter was generated by accumulating responses at base-rate for each minute in the procedure. As can be seen, contingent subjects at each age exhibited gradually accelerating response functions which for all age groups eventually exceeded expected rates of response. In the case of 10-week-olds, however, non-contingent controls exhibited increments similar to contingent subjects. In the two older groups, non-contingent controls performed at or below the expected curve.

Arm-pull measures that eliminate the effects of length of session were employed in subsequent analyses to determine whether learning had occurred. These were average rate, peak response and the number of subjects who attained a response rate 2·5 times baseline.

Average rate. Average arm rate is the total arm-pull frequency divided by the number of minutes in the session. Figure 3a depicts the mean arm rate per minute by age and condition. There were no effects of sex. There was a significant difference between conditions ($F = 13·94$, d.f. $= 1,24$, $P < 0·001$). The average rate of contingent subjects exceeded that of non-contingent controls. There was also a significant age effect ($F = 3·78$, d.f. $= 2,24$, $P < 0·05$), such that 24-week-old subjects had a higher average arm-pull rate per minute than other groups. There was also a significant age × condition interaction ($F = 5·92$, d.f. $= 2,27$, $P < 0·007$) In addition, 24-week-old contingent subjects attained a significantly greater average arm-pull rate per minute than non-contingent controls (Scheffé, $P < 0·05$). The difference between conditions approached significance at 16 weeks (Scheffé, $P < 0·10$) while there was no difference between contingent and non-contingent subjects in the case of 10-week-olds. Further analysis indicated that there was no difference in average arm-pull rate among non-contingent controls, but that 24-week-old contingent subjects had significantly greater average rates than both 16- and 10-week-old subjects (Scheffé, $P_s < 0·05$).

Average response rate constitutes a conservative index of learning since it sums equally across session minutes during which response rates are quite variable. If pre-learning time is long, with response increments sustained only briefly, the use of average rate may obscure learning effects. Therefore, peak response and the number of subjects who attained or exceeded a criteria of 2·5 times base-rate were also examined.

Peak response. Peak response was defined as the greatest response per minute attained during the stimulus period. Peak points occurred between 3 and 18 minutes into the procedure for over 80 per cent of subjects. Peak response presumably indexes the learning of contingency for individual subjects despite variable session length. If the peak response rates of contingent and non-contingent subjects do not differ, then learning on the part of contingent subjects cannot be assumed. Figure 3b shows peak response by age and group. Analyses revealed a significant effect of condition ($F = 21·14$, d.f. $= 1,24$, $P < 0·001$), with contingent subjects exhibiting greater peak response (Scheffé, $P < 0·01$). Significant effects were also obtained for age ($F = 5·98$, d.f. $= 2,24$, $P < 0·007$) and age × condition ($F = 11·34$, d.f. $= 2, 24$, $P < 0·001$). The interaction revealed no condition effects for 10-week-olds; however, 16- and 24-week-old contingent subjects had significantly greater peak rates than their non-contingent counterparts (Scheffé, $P_s < 0·01$ for each).

There were significant age effects within the contingent group, with 24-week-old contingent subjects attaining significantly greater peak response than 16- or 10-week-olds ($F = 10·21$, $P < 0·001$; Scheffé, both $P_s < 0·01$). There were no differences in peak rates among the non-contingent groups. The significant condition × age effect indicates, first, that 16- and 24-week-olds, but not 10-week-olds, show a difference in degree of response

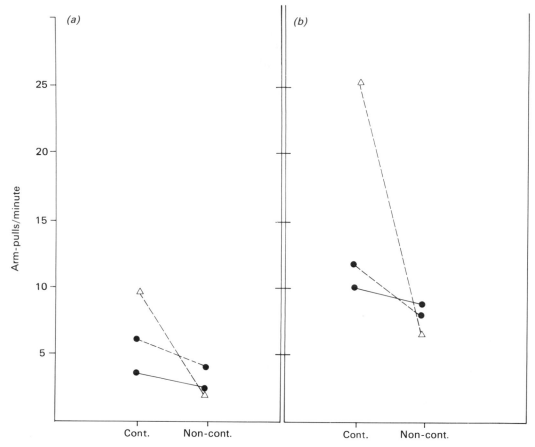

Figure 3. Arm-pull rates (*a*) average and (*b*) peak. ●——●, at 10 weeks; ●---●, at 16 weeks; △---△, at 24 weeks.

between conditions and, second, that when there is a contingency between response and outcome there are age effects, but in the absence of a contingency all ages perform similarly. These two results are consistent with those reported by Millar (1972) who examined pulling responses of 5- and 7-month-old subjects across baseline and two three-minute periods of stimulation. Millar reported age, condition and interaction effects. The interaction indicated 'dramatic effects' of contingent stimulation for the 7-month-old subjects; younger subjects also appeared to learn but less effectively. As in the present study there were no age effects under non-contingent stimulation.

Number of subjects reaching criterion.   If peak rate represents learning, then not only *mean* response should distinguish contingent subjects from non-contingent controls, but a greater number of contingent subjects would be expected to attain peak rates exceeding a particular criterion. The number of subjects in each group who exceeded their base-rate by a factor of 2·5 or more was determined and subjected to chi-square analyses (d.f. = 1) to test for condition effects. Significantly more contingent than non-contingent subjects attained a peak response rate which was at least 2·5 times baseline ($\chi^2 = 9·1$, $P < 0·005$). This effect also occurred within each age group (10 weeks: $\chi^2 = 6·67$, $P < 0·01$; 16 weeks: $\chi^2 = 6·64$, $P < 0·01$; 24 weeks: $\chi^2 = 3·86$, $P = 0·05$). These results indicate that at each age significantly more contingent than non-contingent subjects attained a peak rate 2·5 times their base-rate.

Smiling

The rate of smiling (total number of smiles/total minutes in session) seemed low (contingent: $\overline{X} = 0.56$, SD 1.5; non-contingent: $\overline{X} = 0.58$, SD 1.7). Because of the low rate of smiling and the large differences in variance within age, non-parametric tests were used to examine rates of responding. Although 10-week-old contingent and non-contingent subjects showed no difference in smiling rate, 16- and 24-week-old contingent subjects exhibited greater rates of smiling than their non-contingent counterparts (Wilcoxon $P < 0.05$ for each). The low rate of smiling may in part be a function of the single session used in the present study. Previous studies have reported that smiling occurs in the course of repeated contingency sessions. The present results indicate that smiling is more likely even within a single session in subjects who learn compared with control subjects.

Fussing

Crying was one of the criteria for terminating the session and almost all subjects cried by the end. However, the number of subjects who cried other than at the end was small. Significantly more non-contingent controls than contingent subjects fussed at least once during the sessions, other than in the final minute (χ^2, $P < 0.05$). When the proportion of time spent fussing (fuss time/total time in session) by all subjects was examined, fuss/crying time declined with age for contingent subjects and increased with age for non-contingent controls (excluding the last minute). The proportions were consistently greater for non-contingent controls at each age. The mean proportion for contingent subjects was 0.02 (SD 0.018) while the mean proportion for non-contingent controls was 0.04 (SD 0.035). Standard parametric analyses could not be undertaken since the data was not normally distributed. A Wilcoxon test revealed that non-contingent controls spent proportionally more time fussing than did contingent subjects (Wilcoxon, $P < 0.05$).

Attention

Attention was defined as the average number of seconds spent attending per minute in the session. There were no condition effects. The average number of seconds of attending per minute revealed an age effect ($F = 13.8$, d.f. $= 2,24$, $P < 0.001$) such that 10-week-olds fixated more per minute than the two older age groups (Scheffé, $Ps < 0.05$). Both contingent and non-contingent subjects consistently attended the stimulus across session minutes, but the 10-week-olds averaged more time per minute attending.

Discussion

The present data show the impact of contingent stimulation on the affective–motivational state of the young infant. Lewis (Lewis & Goldberg, 1969; Lewis, 1978; Brinker & Lewis, 1982b) and others (e.g. R. White, 1959; Watson, 1972) have argued that being in control should have powerful emotional/motivational consequences. Moreover, there has been some evidence linking the occurrence of 'natural' contingencies in the infant's social environment (measures of maternal contingent responsivity) to the development of certain social and cognitive competencies (Lewis, 1980; Lewis & Coates, 1980; Coates & Lewis, 1984). Although it is not known whether more contingency experience results in greater competence or the competent child elicits more contingent behaviour from its parents, the present study suggests that it is the contingent stimulation itself which results in a child who is more involved and interested in its environment, factors which should also promote subsequent competence.

Other laboratory evidence with older infants also suggests a connection between affective/motivational states and contingency experience. Gunnar (1980) reported that the experience of control may serve to modulate the potentially distressing effects of an arousing toy. Infants permitted to control the toy's actions exhibited fewer distress responses and were more willing to approach the toy than infants who lacked control. Similarly, Levitt (1980) reported that when initial appearance of a stranger was controlled by the infant, the stranger was responded to more positively during the intrusive stranger approach sequence. The experience of control serves to modulate a potentially distressful social experience as well.

Similar results have been reported in experimental settings with subjects of various ages. McDonnell & Stack (1984) reported recently that contingent subjects between 6 and 24 weeks of age were less fussy and 'more comfortable' than non-contingent subjects in their procedure. In their study, myoelectric responses of the arm were conditioned by means of an overhead mobile. Another recent study has replicated Watson's (1972) report of a link between emotion and learning in a retarded infant. Brinker & Lewis (1982*b*) observed affective change in young handicapped children in an intervention programme designed systematically to provide contingency experience. In two children with visual impairment, one a premature infant with severe retinal damage (4 months postnatal age) and the second a 2-year-old multiply handicapped and severely delayed child diagnosed as cortically blind, contingent audio-visual stimulation was apparently associated with increased eye opening and head raising. Prior to the contingency intervention, both children tended to keep their eyelids semiclosed and chins down, giving them an uninterested, sleepy facial appearance. During the time that each was exposed to a contingency, they were observed to keep their eyes wide open and heads erect, although these behaviours were never directly reinforced. The appearance of such behaviour in children who subsequently exhibited more traditional evidence of learning, together with other facial and postural changes (i.e. leaning forward in the apparatus and smiling) suggested the alert interest of these children in the contingent condition. Such behaviours may be termed affective or motivational and may naturally accompany the learning process.

Age differences in both measures of emotion and contingency learning were evident in the present study. Age and age × condition effects for the average and the peak response measures suggest that the 10-week-old group showed no learning relative to the older age groups. Moreover, the cumulative response curves indicated that both contingent and non-contingent 10-week-olds showed the same pattern of arm-pulling. There were few differences in emotional behaviour observed between 10-week-old contingent and non-contingent subjects except that contingent infants at this age, like their older counterparts, stayed in the task significantly longer than controls. On the other hand, more contingent than non-contingent 10-week-olds exhibited peak rates 2·5 times baseline and 10-week-old contingent subjects accumulated more responses than would be expected had they continued to respond at base-rate. The most parsimonious explanation is that, in this task, 10-week-olds did not learn and therefore showed little emotional behaviour. This linkage between no learning and lack of affect may support the notion of an association between affect and learning by its absence. The 16- and 24-week-olds show both consistent evidence of learning and an emotional response pattern which includes smiling, more time in the procedure and less fussiness.

The pattern of age differences in arm-pulling observed for contingent subjects is consistent with that reported by Rovee-Collier & Fagen (1981) and Millar (1972) and thus is not a procedural artifact. Such age differences can reflect either young infants' inability to process this type of contingency information effectively, immaturity of the particular instrumental response (pulling or kicking), or both factors. The work of McDonnell & Stack (1984) suggests that the nature of the reinforcement is not the sole factor in these apparent age differences in arm response. In their paradigm, myoelectrical responses of the arm and wrist of infants produced conjugate rotation of an overhead mobile. Despite the apparently lesser effort involved in responding contrasted with the present procedure, and the conjugate nature of the contingency, similar age effects were obtained. Infants aged

5–14 weeks of age apparently did not learn as well as older subjects. While it is premature to draw a conclusion at this juncture, this replication of the results given here suggests that the factors responsible for the age differences may lie in the nature of the arm response rather than in the type of reinforcement or in a lesser ability to learn. Lipsitt (1982) has argued that the period between 8 and 16 weeks represents 'a major transitional phase for the learned embellishment and voluntary expression of many reflexes'. Given that reaching and grasping responses undergo major developmental transition during the period under investigation, the use of contingency procedures to facilitate arm movement seems unlikely to achieve this particular goal within a single training session, prior to 16 weeks of age. This is not to say that 10-week-olds are incapable of learning or that repeated exposure to the contingency, such as that employed by Davis & Rovee-Collier (1983) who used two training sessions, might not result in more dramatic evidence of learning. In the present study, however, providing the younger learners individually with presumably optimal time to experience the contingency failed to eliminate age differences in response.

What evidence is there for a link between learning, stimulation and emotion? The evidence suggests that learning is associated (at least for the two older groups) with a particular pattern of emotional behaviour. The comparison between contingency and non-contingency eliminated stimulation level *per se* as a determinant of these emotional responses. The difference obtained between non-contingent and contingent groups on the affective measures indicates that stimulation rate *per se* is an unlikely explanation for these and suggests that emotional behaviour is an important aspect of response change associated with contingent stimulation. Older non-contingent controls not only did not exhibit the degree of elevated response levels of contingent subjects, but they may have found the procedure mildy aversive because they fussed more. As described earlier, control subjects began to drop out of the session after the fourth minute. Though almost all infants cried to criterion at the end of their sessions, fussing during the session was most likely to occur among non-contingent babies, particularly the youngest babies. Short session lengths and increased fussiness may have resulted because control babies were unable to tolerate an unpredictable situation. Consequently, it is important to distinguish between two features of an environment: its stimulation level and its contingent nature (Lewis & Coates, 1980).

The results from both laboratory and natural interaction studies lend credence to the notion that infants are especially responsive to the relationship between their behaviour and environmental occurrences (Watson, 1977; Rovee-Collier & Gekoski, 1979; Papousek & Papousek, 1981; Brinker & Lewis, 1982a). Learning a contingency results in or is accompanied by changes in affective behaviour. Moreover, some emotional effects may appear during or even prior to the demonstration of an increased operant—a result consistent with the view of cognition and affect advanced by Zajonc (1980). Although it may be difficult, if not impossible, to separate the effects of cognition and motivation (Ulvund, 1980; Lewis *et al.*, 1984), the interaction between emotional responses and cognitive events as they evolve needs to be examined in more detail with a variety of measures and in a variety of contexts. Such investigations may lead to a comprehensive model of the relationship between emotion and cognition in the young infant as well as to improved assessment and intervention strategies.

Acknowledgements

This research was supported by the Bureau of Education for the Handicapped, DHEW/OE Contract 300-77-0307 to M. L. and by NICHD Grant no. RD23-HD17205 to M. W. S. We gratefully acknowledge the contribution of Elizabeth Hartka who collected and prepared the data. Portions of these data were presented by E. Hartka and M. Lewis at the Annual Meeting of the Eastern Psychological Association, April 1981.

References

Brinker, R. P. & Lewis, M. (1982*a*). Contingency intervention in infancy. In J. Anderson & J. Cox (eds), *Curriculum Materials for High Risk and Handicapped Infants*. Chapel Hill, NC: Technical Assistance Development Systems.

Brinker, R. P. & Lewis, M. (1982*b*). Discovering the competent handicapped infant: A process approach to assessment and intervention. *Topics in Early Childhood Special Education*, **2**, 1–16.

Coates, D. L. & Lewis, M. (1984). Early mother–infant interaction and infant cognitive status as predictors of school performance and cognitive behaviour in 6-year-olds. *Child Development*, **55**, 1219–1230.

Davis, J. & Rovee-Collier, C. K. (1983). Alleviated forgetting of a learned contingency in 8-week-old infants. *Developmental Psychology*, **19**, 353–365.

Gunnar, M. R. (1980). Control, warning signals and distress in infancy. *Developmental Psychology*, **16**, 281–289.

Kagan, J. (1974). Discrepancy, temperament and infant distress. In M. Lewis & L. A. Rosenblum (eds), *The Origins of Fear*. New York: Wiley.

Lazarus, R. S. (1982). Thoughts on the relations between emotion and cognition. *American Psychologist*, **37**, 1019–1024.

Levitt, M. (1980). Contingent feedback, familiarization, and infant affect: How a stranger becomes a friend. *Developmental Psychology*, **16**, 425–432.

Lewis, M. (1978). The infant and its caregiver: The role of contingency. *Allied Health and Behavioral Sciences*, **1**, 469–492.

Lewis, M. (1980). Developmental theories. In I. L. Kutash & L. B. Schlesinger (eds), *The Handbook on Stress and Anxiety*. San Francisco: Jossey-Bass.

Lewis, M. & Coates, D. L. (1980). Mother–infant interactions and cognitive development in twelve-week-old infants. *Infant Behavior and Development*, **3**, 95–105.

Lewis, M. & Goldberg, S. (1969). Perceptual–cognitive development in infancy: A generalized expectancy model as a function of the mother–infant interaction. *Merrill–Palmer Quarterly*, **15**, 81–100.

Lewis, M. & Michalson, L. (1983). *Children's Emotions and Moods: Developmental Theory and Assessment*. New York: Plenum.

Lewis, M., Sullivan, M. W. & Michalson, L. (1984). The cognitive–emotional fugue. In C. Izard, J. Kagan & R. Zajonc (eds), *Emotion, Cognition and Behavior*. New York: Cambridge University Press.

Lipsitt, L. (1982). Infant learning. In T. Field, A. Huston, L. Troll, H. Quay & G. Finley (eds), *Review of Human Development*. New York: Wiley.

McDonnell, P. & Stack, D. (1984) Conditioning of 4- to 6-month-old infants by means of myoelectrically controlled reinforcement. Presentation at the International Infancy Conference, New York City, April.

Millar, W. S. (1972). A study of operant conditioning under delayed reinforcement in early infancy. *Monographs of the Society for Research in Child Development*, **37**(2), Serial no. 147.

Papousek, H. & Papousek, M. (1981). The common in the uncommon: Comments on the child's integrative capacities and on initiative parenting. In M. Lewis & L. A. Rosenblum (eds), *The Uncommon Child: The Genesis of Behavior*, vol. 3. New York: Plenum.

Rovee-Collier, C. K. & Fagen, J. W. (1976). Extended conditioning and 24-hour retention in infants. *Journal of Experimental Child Psychology*, **21**, 1–11.

Rovee-Collier, C. K. & Fagen, J. W. (1981). The retrieval of memory in early infancy. In L. P. Lipsitt (ed.), *Advances in Infancy Research*, vol. 1. Norwood, NJ: Ablex.

Rovee-Collier, C. K. & Gekoski, M. J. (1979). The economics of infancy: A review of conjugate reinforcement. In H. W. Reese & L. P. Lipsitt (eds), *Advances in Child Development and Behavior Research*, vol. 13. New York: Academic Press.

Seligman, M. (1975). *Helplessness: On Depression, Development and Death*. San Francisco: Freeman.

Sullivan, M. W. (1982). Reactivation: Priming forgotten memories in human infants. *Child Development*, **53**, 516–523.

Sullivan, M. W., Rovee-Collier, C. K. & Tynes, D. (1979). A conditioning analysis of long-term memory in 3-month-old infants. *Child Development*, **50**, 152–162.

Ulvund, S. E. (1980). Cognition and motivation in early infancy: An interactionistic approach. *Human Development*, **23**, 17–32.

Uzgiris, I. C. & Hunt, J. McV. (1970). Attentional preference and experience: An exploratory longitudinal study of the effect of familiarity and responsiveness. *Journal of Genetic Psychology*, **117**, 109–121.

Watson, J. S. (1972). Smiling, cooing and the game. *Merrill–Palmer Quarterly*, **18**, 323–329.

Watson, J. S. (1977). Perception of contingency as a determinant of social responsiveness. In E. B. Thoman (ed.), *Origins of Infant Social Responsiveness*. Hillsdale, NJ: Erlbaum.

White, B. L., Castle, P. & Held, R. (1964). Observations on the development of visually directed reaching. *Child Development*, **35**, 349–364.

White, R. (1959). Motivation reconsidered: The concept of competence. *Psychological Review*, **66**, 297–334.

Zajonc, R. B. (1980). Feeling and thinking: Preferences need no inferences. *American Psychologist*, **35**, 151–175.

Requests for reprints should be addressed to M. Lewis, Professor of Pediatrics, Rutgers Medical School, Medical Education Building CN-19, New Brunswick, NJ 08903, USA.

Margaret Wolan Sullivan is also at the above address.

Jeanne Brooks-Gunn is at the Educational Testing Service, Princeton, NJ.

British Journal of Developmental Psychology (1985), **3**, 317–320   *Printed in Great Britain*

Book reviews

Born Too Soon: Preterm Birth and Early Development. *By* Susan Goldberg & Barbara A. DiVitto. San Francisco: Freeman. 1983. Pp. 201. £5.80.

Following a quarter of a century of intensive research with the normal term new-born, there is now a shift of interest towards babies born at risk. As medical advances progressively reduce mortality, morbidity emerges as a more serious problem, and as the physical consequences of premature birth diminish we can afford to take account of the psychological aftermath. Such is our system of priorities, and it has led to the emergence of a wish for solid information about the consequences of prematurity from both parents and professionals. This thoughtful and well-written little book is designed to fill that need, but it may not be most suitable for its primary audience: the parents of pre-term babies.

The authors work systematically through the issues raised by pre-term birth. A description of intensive care units is followed by three chapters reviewing what is known about the motor, cognitive, and social functioning and development of pre-term babies. The book does an excellent job of providing a clear account of both statistical and experimental methodological issues which makes the essentials of the rationale easily understandable. The findings are seen as indicating that pre-term birth does not necessarily lead to subsequent impairment though there are likely to be effects in the short term: conclusions with which most workers in this area would agree. The next chapter reviews the short-term effects to show that they operate rather consistently to make care giving 'more work and less fun'. There is a sensitive account of the emotional upset that a premature baby may cause and a certain amount of reassurance is provided. Parents, however, are likely to feel let down by the absence of any content that would tell them clearly what to do for the best. Next, intervention programmes are reviewed to show that a variety of regimens can result in improvements, but it is stressed that these are group effects and that the optimal care for any individual baby needs to be agreed between the physician, the family and the infant. The final summary attempts to indicate the complexity of causal processes in determining the outcome of early birth but does not offer a model that could deal adequately with the influence of the baby on the care-giving environment.

As the authors state, this is not a book about how to care for a pre-term baby, and parents are likely to learn from it rather less than they want to know about what to do, and rather more than they want to know about the methods and objectives of psychological research. Specialists in this area will find little that will be new to them but a few things to quarrel with. For example, prematurity is defined in terms of both gestation and birth weight in the Introduction, but the book deals only with pre-term birth. The often more serious issue of 'low weight for date' babies is never mentioned. Between the lay reader and the specialist there is quite a large readership who could find it useful. For many psychologists it will provide a brief and readable account of an area that is becoming increasingly important to developmentalists. For non-psychologists who are working with pre-term babies·and their parents it provides an accessible and authoritative survey of relevant psychological work which could be a basis for a more scientific approach to planning practice. Many readers will find the glossary useful, but few will be helped by a system of referencing that is quite unnecessarily complicated, and British readers may be discomfited by the North American bias ('follow-up treatment is rarely free'). In sum, this is a successful exercise in making accessible to a wider public a clear account of what research has been done with pre-term babies, why it had to be done in that way, and what conclusions can be drawn using appropriate measures of caution and optimism.

PETER STRATTON

The Social and Mental Life of Babies. *By* Kenneth Kaye. London: Methuen. 1984.

This book is a broad theoretical statement about psychological development in infancy and, as the subtitle *How Parents Create Persons* implies, it is a theory rooted in the idea that cognitive development is a product of social processes and parental influences, albeit of a subtle kind. A particularly interesting aspect of the work is that a large proportion of the empirical data that Kaye uses to support or illustrate his position is drawn from studies of the structure and dynamics of parent–infant interaction, and often studies using micro- and sequential analysis. It is probably the most ambitious attempt to date to draw this kind of data into a general conceptual framework within developmental psychology.

Kaye is much attracted by general systems theory as a framework in which to consider the complexities of development and social life, and this is one of the best attempts known to the reviewer to use this framework without befuddling the reader with extremely abstract concepts which seem to clarify the issues not at all—least of all in relation to the interpretation of empirical data. One key idea that Kaye sets out to clarify concerns the sense or senses in which the parent–infant relationship might usefully be considered as a *system*. In recent years, two facts in particular have led to an emphasis on the *complexity* of early social interaction. Infants are now known to be capable of well-organized behaviour from very early in life, and parent–infant interaction is known to be a two-way affair, with parental behaviour being contingent on infant behaviour as well as the other way around. Kaye argues against drawing the conclusion from this that the parent–infant dyad is more than the sum of its parts, and it is therefore not considered useful to conceive of such a dyad as a social system. For Kaye, two individuals must have shared purposes and a shared developmental history (as opposed to a shared evolutionary history) in order to be considered a social system. The latter criterion rules out, unfortunately, as a matter of definition, any possibility that dyads involving very young infants could exhibit the properties of a social system.

Kaye uses this framework to examine some of his own data on diverse facets of parent–infant interaction. And he also uses it to examine the continuity issue. He fails to find good evidence of continuity in *dyadic* factors, as opposed to continuities in parental characteristics.

How then does Kaye see the infant as becoming part of a social system in relationship with his/her parents? Basically he takes a Vygotskyan view. He sees the infant serving an apprenticeship, with the parents providing step-at-a-time opportunities for acquiring the skills of social life. Parents are seen as providing much of the overall structure for early interactions, with the infant being encouraged to take the lead only in those parts that he or she can manage. Infants learn how to operate as members of social systems because parents place them in situations where the skills they lack are performed for them. At first, interaction is primarily a matter of the parent fitting in with temporal features of the infant's behaviour—sucking and indications of attention and arousal. Shared intentions develop gradually, followed by shared memories and, in turn, shared language. Kaye makes some strong claims for human uniqueness for the whole of this process, even prior to the emergence of language. He attaches great importance to the suck–pause pattern of human neonates, which is not, apparently, paralleled in other mammals. This pattern exists in humans, he claims, simply to prompt mothers into responding to this temporal aspect of the infant's behaviour. This is the first stage of an apprenticeship to social life that is claimed to be without parallel among other species. Claims of well-developed social competence very early in life are, however, firmly rejected.

Kaye believes that mothers' responses to the pauses during sucking by neonates are the earliest manifestation of the phenomenon of turn taking, having a clear developmental connection with conversational turn taking. In fact, a diverse array of non-verbal interactional patterns is seen as falling under the rubric of turn taking so that one is left wondering whether any of the interpersonal contingencies in early social interaction are *not* forms of turn taking.

Verbal turn taking is seen as the very essence of communicative interaction and the functioning of human social systems. However, Kaye argues at considerable length against the views that there is symbolicity before language. Participation in various preverbal interactional routines is thought to guide the apprentice toward symbolic communication, but it is not reasonable to conceive of inter-subjectivity before language. The arguments against claims of very early inter-subjectivity are particularly compelling, but there comes a point where Kaye's arguments become so heavily definitional that one begins to tire. Nonetheless, there are some interesting and carefully thought through distinctions drawn here.

If parental behaviour, shaped by evolution, is the mainspring of psychological development, then development might be expected to be rather variable in the face of diverse patterns of parenting. The tenets of general systems theory concerning resistance to perturbations can be invoked in an attempt to explain why development seems to be fairly resilient, yet with all its ambiguities and practical problems, data on the influence of parental behaviour on developmental outcomes will probably be the ultimate arbiter of the usefulness of this approach. In a related vein, a view of development being drawn along by parental influence inevitably endows some with an enthusiasm for trying to make things work even better. Happily, Kaye is cool about the prospects of willy-nilly intervention. His final chapter is a cautious and well-balanced consideration of the uses that might be made of the insights revealed by recent ideas on parent–infant interaction.

I like this book for the careful development of arguments and presentation of the theory in a way that does not depart too far from the realms of empirical research. The paperback edition, published just two years after the hardback, is most welcome.

GLYN COLLIS

Advances in Infancy Research, vol. 2. *Edited by* L. P. Lipsitt. Norwood, NJ: Ablex. 1983. £29.95. ISBN 0 89391 113 5.

Advances in Infancy Research is a parallel publication to the journal *Infant Behavior and Development*, and is designed as a forum for articles that describe extensive research programmes or provide integrative reviews of particular areas. Although chapters are mainly invited, the normal journal review process applies to all contributions. Consequently, this publication lies somewhere between a journal and an edited book. No explicit theme binds together the contributions, so the reader is likely to encounter a diverse selection of topics within the same volume. Volume 2 is no exception. After an introduction by Harriet Rheingold entitled 'The social and socializing infant', chapters follow on the structure of mind in infancy (Butterworth), recognition memory as a measure of intelligence (Fagan & Singer), category detection (Reznick & Kagan), development of manual behaviour (Lockman & Ashmead), object search (Schuberth), intermodal perception and language development (Sullivan & Horowitz), direct perception (von Hofsten), and imitation (Meltzoff & Moore). This diversity makes the volume hard to review in a succinct fashion, since the only way to do full justice to the contributions would be to review each separately. Instead, I have attempted to give a general feel for the volume, picking out any general themes that seemed to be emerging.

Many of the chapters are heavily laden with data, and I came away feeling I had learned a lot about the current state of knowledge about infant abilities. But at times there seemed to be lack of theoretical evaluation of these findings, or at least there did not seem to be a clear story that placed them within the context of development in general. At the end of their chapter, Sullivan & Horowitz write, 'The temptation is great to make predictions and develop a theoretical framework . . .', but add '. . . we prefer to defer picking up this gauntlet until sufficient empirical support is available to guide theoretical speculation.' I wish that they had thrown caution to the wind here, since the discipline will probably progress more swiftly through testing theoretical speculations than through the laborious process of accumulating evidence. Von Hofsten gives a good indication of the importance of theory in directing research in making the point that from the standpoint of Gibsonian theory, the use of artificial stimuli can lead to underestimation of infants' capabilities. The theory predicts that any pre-adapted mechanisms for extracting information from the environment should be adapted to information that is ecologically relevant to the infant. But theories also have to adapt themselves to the data, and a possible weakness of von Hofsten's thesis is apparent in his noting how remarkable it is that ecologically irrelevant stimuli evoke any systematic responses at all. We should be wary of pre-judging ecological relevance, something that must be in part an empirical question, and it would seem that an important test of ecological theorizing is the comparison of ability across supposed ecologically relevant and irrelevant tasks.

The contrast between chapters with a predominantly methodological slant and those with a more theoretical orientation is fairly noticeable. But both types of chapter have important messages. Reznick & Kagan's chapter on category detection is largely devoted to a technical evaluation of methodologies, and they present strong arguments for refinement of methodology and, where possible, multiple methods of measuring the same abilities. Sullivan & Horowitz, without becoming heavily involved in theory, argue for the importance of multimodal stimulation for early language development. Another chapter that makes important links with later abilities is the one by Fagan & Singer, in which strong arguments are presented in favour of infant recognition memory as a superior predictor of future intelligence than more conventional sensorimotor scales. Also, in some chapters there are examples of the way in which theorizing confined to a particular domain can have implications for grander developmental theorizing. For instance, Lockman & Ashmead's argument is that, rather than possessing a general mapping of visual to motor space, infants are capable of coordinations that are specific to different levels of manual behaviour. This raises the general question of how perception relates to action in development.

Other chapters (e.g. Butterworth's and Schuberth's) are devoted more to theoretical evaluation in relation to what currently appears to be a more messy data-base. However, Meltzoff & Moore combine both theoretical and methodological evaluation, arguing that some sort of standardization of methodology is required if theories of imitation in infancy are to proceed. This is an important point, since it seems that the areas that are richest in theoretical terms are often the ones with the weakest empirical base. In some cases these areas could benefit from the methodological rigour applied in the more empirically driven areas of study. This may not be easy to achieve, particularly if the theory demands that experimentation should become ecologically relevant, but the problem should not be dodged and what we badly need are methods that combine ecological relevance with methodological rigour.

Another theme that emerged was a noticeable attention to social competence in infancy. Rheingold provides a view of a socially competent infant, and a number of other chapters link cognitive development to social competence in one way or another. For instance, Butterworth accommodates fascinating evidence of joint visual attention in infancy within his theory of early perception. Sullivan & Horowitz put multimodal perception in the context of early parent–infant interaction, and Meltzoff & Moore apply a cognitive analysis to infant imitation.

In summary, this is a diverse set of papers, and as such is an important source of theoretical and empirical information on infancy. I would not describe it as bedtime reading—some of the more technical chapters made fairly heavy reading, mainly because there seemed to be no strong story running through them—but I would recommend it as a reference book for the sheer amount of information that it contains.

GAVIN BREMNER

The Development of Infants Born at Risk. *By* Deborah L. Holmes, Jill Nagy Reich & Joseph F. Pasternak. Hillsdale, NJ/London: Erlbaum. Pp. 257. ISBN: 0 89859 283 6.

The authors of this book have undertaken the difficult task of unravelling the complex relationship between events occuring prenatally, intra-natally and postnatally, and the subsequent development of the infant and child. They tackle this task by first providing a comprehensive (although in places rather sketchy) background to the vast amount of research in this area. In the space of a few chapters, they define the 'at risk infant', outline foetal brain development and deal with many aspects of current obstetric and neonatal care. In places the patho-physiological explanations and clinical details are somewhat 'simplistic', but nevertheless provide sufficient working background for those not directly involved in perinatal care.

However, the main feature of this book is the critical evaluation of current research in the behavioural–developmental field particularly as it relates to the high risk infant. Throughout, the authors emphasize the difficulties of interpreting the vast quantity of data that has been collected over the years. This is due to differing methodologies, subject selection and varying outcome measures. Hence we and the authors are confronted with a welter of 'inconclusive data and ambiguous results'. In particular, the authors emphasize the shortcomings of retrospective studies which attempt to correlate perinatal events and outcome. They urge that prospective studies be carefully designed with controls and the use of objective tests in the follow-up. They acknowledge the impact of rapidly changing patterns of neonatal care on the interpretation of follow-up findings. And not least, they address the problem of defining 'normality' and levels of disability and handicap. Indeed most of the areas of concern and controversy in this fascinating field are dealt with in this compact book. The references for each chapter are very comprehensive. As reports continue to flow out of units, it is understandably difficult to keep references up to date. However, they provide excellent background resource material for any researcher in this area.

The final chapter which provides a critical appraisal of intervention programmes is of particular interest. The conclusions which can be drawn from the reported programmes are very limited. Most studies have no controls and do not attempt to 'remediate' specific deficits but rather provide a 'general enrichment programme'. As the authors point out, a good deal more needs to be known of the state organization of infants, their sensory thresholds and their capacity to process information, before more specific interventions can be devised and their effectiveness properly tested. So this interesting and thoughtful book poses more questions than it answers. It would have been very useful perhaps to have a short chapter outlining appropriate methodologies and strategies which could be used to obtain more conclusive and meaningful data, but overall it is a book to be recommended to all those involved in the follow-up of high risk infants.

MARGARET ANN JOHNSON

Index*

*Page numbers all refer to the number in square brackets at the head of each page.

Journals of The British Psychological Society